P9-BYH-018

Death by
PowerPoint

❖

Also by Michael Flocker

The Metrosexual Guide to Style

The Hedonism Handbook

The Fame Game

Death by PowerPoint
A Modern Office Survival Guide

MICHAEL FLOCKER

DA CAPO PRESS
A Member of the Perseus Books Group

Many of the designations used by manufacturers and sellers to distinguish their products are claimed as trademarks. Where those designations appear in this book and Da Capo Press was aware of a trademark claim, those designations have been printed with initial capital letters.

Copyright © 2006 by Michael Flocker

All rights reserved. No part of this publication may be reproduced, stored in a retrieval system, or transmitted, in any form or by any means, electronic, mechanical, photocopying, recording, or otherwise, without the prior written permission of the publisher. Printed in the United States of America.

Cataloging-in-Publication data for this book is available from the Library of Congress.

Text design and illustrations by Jon Resh / Undaunted Design Co.
Author photo by Lauren Dobkin

First Da Capo Press edition 2006
ISBN-13: 978-0-306-81512-6
ISBN-10: 0-306-81512-5

Published by Da Capo Press
A member of the
Perseus Books Group
http://www.dacapopress.com

Da Capo Press books are available at special discounts for bulk purchases in the U.S. by corporations, institutions, and other organizations. For more information, please contact the Special Markets Department at the Perseus Books Group, 11 Cambridge Center, Cambridge, MA 02142, or call (800) 255-1514 or (617) 252-5298, or e-mail special.markets@perseusbooks.com.

1 2 3 4 5 6 7 8 9—09 08 07 06

Contents

Introduction

CAN YOU IMAGINE HOW HORRENDOUS IT must have been to live at the lower rungs of society during medieval times? Just think of it. Aside from the plagues, the stench, and the crazy superstitions there was a tremendous amount of injustice. All those riches, all that land and all the power were concentrated in the hands of very few. So while the kings and queens lounged about in their ivory towers hoarding all the wealth, the peasants and the serfs toiled in the fields and then had the added indignity of having to pay taxes on the land they farmed to the landowners themselves. These would have been serious grounds for disgruntlement.

Of course, in a class society the very fact that the aristocracy owns and controls the land is the reason they are able to enjoy their riches and exploit the peasants as the proverbial shit was shoveled on their behalf. Granted, the whole notion does have a certain appeal if you happen to be the one in the castle, but for those below, well, that's the kind of thing that brings about revolutions.

It's amazing to think that the feudal system lasted as long as it did. Is it any wonder that the masses eventually rose up in a global crime spree of beheadings, murders, and assassinations? Well, it was really just a matter of physics, if you think about it. Any system that gets too top-heavy eventually has to roll over on its back, right?

Of course, as history steamrolled along, the toppling of the royal houses ushered in a chaotic century of competing ideologies, crazy tyrants, international espionage, the redrawing of borders, and lots of headaches in general as the masses tried to define and realize their respective utopian ideals. But as the masses were focused on national identities and political doctrines, another silent revolution was already in the making. The power and wealth once held by the aristocracy didn't simply disappear, it was up for grabs, so an old idea reared its head, and the rise of the modern corporation was underway.

The notion of a corporation had emerged as early as the sixteenth century in countries like England and Holland. It was a nifty little social invention whereby the state grants a corporate charter so that private financial resources could be used for public purposes. That meant that corporations were now free to exercise their influence on politics, use the mass media for their own purposes, invest in social development, and pursue a host of other opportunities to increase their wealth and power. As early as 1884 there were some who were frantically waving red flags:

"I see in the near future a crisis approaching that unnerves me and causes me to tremble for the safety of my country . . . corporations have been enthroned and an era of corruption in high places will follow, and the money power of the country will endeavor to prolong its reign by working upon the prejudices of the people until all wealth is aggregated in a few hands and the Republic is destroyed."
>>> U.S. President Abraham Lincoln, Nov. 21, 1864 (letter to Colonel William F. Elkins) Ref: *The Lincoln Encyclopedia*, Archer H. Shaw (Macmillan, 1950, NY).

Apparently Lincoln saw a little further down the road than the rest of his contemporaries. He recognized the potential for greed and corruption early on, but did anyone really listen? It would seem that they didn't. When you consider the ongoing parade in recent years of CEOs posing for mug shots and sporting orange jumpsuits as they slink along the corridors of the Big House, it's clear that his warnings were not so much alarmist as they were prophetic.

Just four short years after Lincoln wrote those words, the U.S. Supreme Court included a ruling in the Fourteenth Amendment to the Constitution, which stated that corporations were to be considered "natural persons" and were therefore entitled to the same rights and protections as an individual. The creation of such "natural persons" paved the way for a new era of Kings and Queens—the corporate ones.

Cut to the twenty-first century and the facts are quite intriguing. According to a 2001 report by the Institute for Policy Studies:

▲ Of the one hundred largest economies in the world, fifty-one are corporations; only forty-nine are countries (based on a comparison of corporate sales and country GDPs).

▲ The Top 200 corporations' combined sales are eighteen times the size of the combined annual income of the 1.2 billion people (24 percent of the total world population) living in "severe" poverty.

▲ While the sales of the Top 200 are the equivalent of 27.5 percent of world economic activity, they employ only 0.78 percent of the world's workforce.

▲ A full 5 percent of the Top 200's combined workforce is employed by Wal-Mart. The discount retail giant is the top private employer in the world, with 1.14 million workers. (In 2003, that number rose to 1.34 million.)

▲ U.S. corporations dominate the Top 200, with eighty-two slots (41 percent of the total). Japanese firms are second, with only forty-one slots.

So, you see, things haven't changed all that much since the medieval days. And here you thought your corporate career was so very modern and fancy. Well, maybe it is, and maybe it's not. But the fact remains that millions upon millions of us now find ourselves employed by international conglomerates and corporate entities. And so, as you sit typing in your little grey cubicle or chant the corporate cheer at your morning meeting, economic borders and cultural identities are quickly dissipating as corporate logos replace national flags and indigenous youths in the Amazon Basin are sporting Nike sneakers.

But one can only spend so much time thinking about the larger ramifications of such things. For those incensed about the evils of the global economy there are a lot of worthy organizations to join that give voice to the disenfranchised and are working hard to "stick it to the man." But for many of us who have unwittingly found ourselves "inside the machine," it's the daily aggravations, the ridiculous rituals, and the idiotic idiosyncrasies of corporate culture that impact us most. How does one survive day-to-day in the precarious and preposterous atmosphere of corporate life? Whether you work at a massive corporate "compound" or a small satellite office, the daily grind can be utterly soul-crushing.

Then again, in the bigger picture, it's just a job, right? You're not actually shoveling shit in a field, and for that you should be grateful. And if you're really not up for triggering a full-scale revolution, then you simply need to make the most of the situation without letting it get you down. With a balanced perspective, a grain of salt, and a good sense of humor, pretty much anything is survivable. So, why not start with what is immediately in front of you and within your control?

Like love, working in an office is a messy tangle of outrageous demands, constant compromises, mixed signals, flashes of terror, and occasional moments of ecstacy . . . minus the moments of ecstacy. Even so, it is manageable and it may even bring you some joy, but only if you know how to play the game.

CHAPTER

1

The
Lives of
Drones
and
Workers

"All paid jobs absorb and
degrade the mind."
>>> Aristotle

HHT HHT
HHT HHT HHT
HHT HHT

We Are Not Alone

ANY SOCIETY IS DEFINED AS A VOLUNTARY association of individuals or a cooperative social group that shares a common end. Through organization and working together collective goals and/or needs are met. This definition applies to any number of life forms. In the case of human beings it may apply to nations, towns, corporations, religious sects, minority groups, or any number of other collectives. It also applies to the animal kingdom.

Studies have shown that young male elephants, orphaned by poachers, will band together and wreak havoc, even becoming violent without proper guidance by their elders. Deprived of social order and custom any life form runs the risk of spiraling out of control. And so we organize for the greater good. And with the possible exception of those wildly clever dolphins, it is widely assumed that human beings have created for themselves the most intricate of social structures. Though that may be true, we are hardly the only species to come up with some truly imbalanced hierarchies.

Aristocracy is not the exclusive invention of the human race. And even in the twenty-first century, in which corporate culture is quickly redefining the very definition of global power, as national identity is being usurped by corporate allegiance, there are other models that parallel our increasingly ridiculous state of being. Take for example the case of the honey bee.

Honey Bee Colonies

While bees have extremely small brains, they maintain a very complex social hierarchy that largely revolves around the well-being of a designated "queen." Consider the following facts about life within a bee colony and consider how they might also describe your workplace:

❖ Honey bees have distinct mouthparts designed for both chewing and sucking.

❖ Bees live in small cells or cavities, with crappy paper-like walls that are produced by the collective.

❖ Adult bees all feed off of the honey produced by the workers, but only the queen eats the royal jelly.

❖ A complete colony will consist of roughly 40,000 to 50,000 bees, the vast majority of which do all the work and will die young.

❖ Honey bees are social insects with a very distinct division of labor.

And what of the designated hierarchy? Might these traits also apply?

THE QUEEN

❖ There can be only one queen per hive.

❖ The queen lives much longer than the workers and the drones.

❖ The queen is larger and longer than the other bees, because she is fed an exclusive, lifelong diet of "royal jelly," which is withheld from all other larvae after the first two days of life.

❖ A queen is unable to care for herself and must be surrounded by attendants who feed her, groom her, and carry away her waste.

❖ The queen needs only to mate once with several drones to remain fertile for life.

❖ A fertile queen may lay up to 2,000 eggs per day.

❖ Unlike the worker bees, a queen bee can sting multiple times without any adverse effects.

❖ The queen decides which eggs will be workers and which will be drones.

❖ When a queen dies or becomes infertile, the other bees instinctively create a new queen by selecting a young larva and feeding it only the "royal jelly."

❖ The new queen will find and destroy any rival queens.

Hmm. Interesting.

THE DRONES

❖ The drones are the male bees.

❖ Drone bees are larger than the worker bees, and they have large crossed eyes and no stinger.

❖ Often considered fat and lazy, they lead a life of leisure doing no work whatsoever.

❖ Unable to care for themselves, they are fed by the workers.

❖ Their sole purpose is to fertilize the numerous eggs laid by the queen.

❖ If the colony is short of honey, the drones will often be kicked out.

❖ They either die upon mating or are expelled from the hive as winter approaches.

Sound like anyone you work with?

WORKER BEES

❖ Worker bees are the female bees.

❖ The specialized duties of workers are primarily determined by their age.

❖ The first three days of a worker bee's life are spent cleaning the hive.

DID YOU KNOW?

The three U.S. companies with the largest number of employees in 2003 were:

Wal-Mart: 1,341,500

McDonald's: 413,000

UPS: 365,500

(source: Forbes.com)

❖ They then move on to care for the queen, tend to the eggs and larvae, oversee comb construction, and guard the hive entrance.

❖ Worker bees expend a huge amount of time and energy controlling the temperature of the hive.

❖ Workers often control the fate of the colony by governing the number of eggs laid by the queen and overseeing the production and development of drones.

❖ If a worker impales an adversary just once, she will lose her sting and die shortly thereafter.

Any of that sound familiar?

If anything, it clearly illustrates the simple fact that life is not fair—at least in the workplace. But just because life is unfair, that doesn't mean that the individual is not in control of his or her own fate. The key to a happy and fulfilling life, both in and out of the workplace, lies in the ability to recognize what is and what is not within your control. Your job does not define your life—it is only one part of it. Your greatest weapons in the grand struggle are perspective and appreciation of irony as you chuckle your way up the ladder.

Your Access to the Honeypot

DID YOU KNOW?

In 2005 the collective net worth of the world's 691 billionaires was $2.2 trillion.

(source: Forbes.com)

So, clearly the Queen has the best deal, and the drones and the workers do all the actual work— big surprise. But it's all for the team, right? When company profits go up we all benefit, n'est-ce pas? Well, not exactly. According to the *New York Times*, the average CEO of a major company in 2004 pulled in $9.84 million in compensation. Of course, we all realize that those designer suits, palatial homes, and extravagant vacations can be quite expensive, but the fact is that the money for these exorbitant payouts usually comes directly out of the shareholders' profits and the retirement accounts of the workers.

Maddening? Maybe. But always keep in mind that history has shown us time and again that when things go bad these are the people most likely to be beheaded in the town square. You, on the other hand, will be among the delirious townspeople, clapping and jumping up and down on the sidelines.

THE TOP CONSUMERS OF THE ROYAL JELLY IN 2004

According to *Forbes*, here are the three top-

> "I do not like work even when someone else does it."
>
> >>> Mark Twain

earning CEOs of major companies in 2004, ranked by total compensation:

Yahoo Inc., Terry S. Semel:
>>>**$230,554,000**

InterActiveCorp, Barry Diller:
>>>**$156,186,000**

United Health Group Inc., William W. McGuire:
>>>**$124,774,000**
(Source: *Forbes*)

Just for laughs, if you want to see your own CEO's paycheck from 2004, go to:
www.forbes.com/static/execpay2005/totcomp.html

Of course, a mad rush to revolution is probably not the best of ideas in an already turbulent world, and human nature dictates that the higher we move up in the workplace, the more sympathetic we become to outrageous salaries. Therefore, a calm and measured approach is best as we assess our own predicaments and evaluate our own options.

Your First Clues

So, you're one of the underlings with a salary more than a few digits short of the CEO's and a whole lot of rungs left to climb on the ladder above you. But is the job exactly what you thought it would be? Is the atmosphere of the office, the mindset of the management, and the expectations you face daily quite what you imagined? Probably not.

Chances are there were several telltale signs looming that should have tipped you off when you first applied. The ways in which a corporation or company describes itself and the terminology of the job description are often good indicators of what can be expected. Did you catch the true meanings when you walked in the door?

An Exciting and Rare Opportunity: We expect you to be eternally grateful, humble, and thankful.

A Fast-Paced Environment: We have no time to train or explain. Be prepared to be tossed in the deep end.

Duties Will Vary: Prepare to be buried from day one.

Seeking Motivated Self-Starter: We're not sure what this job is supposed to be, but we expect you to figure it out.

Candidate Should Work Well Under Pressure: The majority of your coworkers will behave in the manner of high-strung, shrieking howler monkeys.

DID YOU KNOW?

In 1980 the average CEO of a major corporation made 42 times the pay of the average worker.

By 1999 the average figure was 419 times the average pay.

— "A Decade of Executive Excess" - Institute for Policy Studies and United For a Fair Economy

Must Be Deadline-Oriented: Everyone else here is supremely disorganized so you will be the one who is held accountable.

Must Exhibit Leadership Skills: You will have the duties of management, but the title of associate underling.

Attention to Detail Essential: We are seeking a magician to compensate for sloppy and lazy coworkers.

Ability to Multitask and Prioritize: All here is chaos and your workload will be unmanageable.

Some Overtime Required: You will be perpetually on call and should begin winding down any personal relationships ASAP.

Casual Workplace Atmosphere: Your salary will be so low that you will not be able to afford a suit.

Seeking Career-Minded Individuals: A life outside the workplace involving travel, social life, or family will not be tolerated.

Tremendous Opportunity for Growth: You'll never leave your desk and your ass will grow huge.

In hindsight it all becomes clear, but dwelling on the past and reflecting on missed signs serves no purpose. If you're inside the machine now, you'll need to focus on where you are, and what you can do to make the sailing a little less turbulent.

Understanding Your Position in the Workplace

The first step to take when attempting to stabilize the waters is to understand your position in the larger hierarchy. Knowing who is above you is just as important as knowing who is below you if there is to be any upward mobility at all. Of course, the employment structure of a mammoth corporation can be—and usually is—about as tangled up as those Christmas lights you shove in the back of the closet each year. It is therefore best to begin with the one directly above you: your boss.

Exactly what kind of boss do you have? Are you friends? Are you enemies? Are you strangers when you pass in the hall, nodding politely with minimal eye contact? In the grand analysis most bosses can be neatly pigeonholed into one of several stereotypes, each of which requires a different form of manipulation and finesse as you mold them to your will. Let us review:

THE FRIEND BOSS

This is the ideal. If a true friendship exists between you and your boss, then respect and good will tends to go in both directions. They will look out for your best interests and you will naturally want to do your best to please them. A united effort emerges without struggle. Though certain ethical boundaries do require discretion and should be adhered to, you will invariably benefit from sage advice and a close-knit trust.

>>>*BEST DEFENSE:* None required. But if you want the friendship to last, make sure your time spent together outside the office involves minimal workplace discussion and focuses on your real lives.

THE BUDDY BOSS

Unlike a "Friend Boss" who actually is your friend, this one *needs* to be your friend. Likely scenarios include ghastly after-work invitations, awkward personal confessions, and a suffocating interest in your personal life. Office gossip, personal anecdotes, and internet jokes will be coming your way like locusts. The upside is that they'll be far more likely to take the fall when you screw up to prevent you from getting in trouble.

>>>*BEST DEFENSE:* Enjoy the convivial atmosphere and low stress without giving too much personal information away. Maintaining some professional boundaries will keep you from getting sucked too deeply into their "issues" and dramas.

THE PANDORA'S BOSS

This would be the emotional train wreck with the wild mood swings. You never know who is going to come flying out of that office. Warm, light-hearted exchanges are juxtaposed with tirades and tantrums that reveal an unnervingly unbalanced psyche. Rarely effective, this boss loves nothing better than assigning blame and having strained confrontations in which employee shortcomings are diplomatically addressed.

>>>*BEST DEFENSE:* An aloof distance is always best when dealing with the emotionally deranged. A nice blend of composure and concern usually works best, and a snappy wardrobe tends to impress such shaky, superficial, and easily distracted basket cases.

THE BULLY BOSS

Always puffed up and ready to find fault, this one uses aggression to unsuccessfully mask deep insecurity. As in the schoolyard a bully must always have a target to pick on and publicly humiliate. One employee is always targeted and singled out as the weak link that is inefficient and "doesn't get it."

>>>*BEST DEFENSE:* Establish early on that you will not be the one to be singled out and bullied, and meet any attempts by the boss to create alliances with cool, intelligent reason. Bullies are almost always emotional and stupid, so a calm demeanor scares the shit out of them.

THE JOCK BOSS

This one thinks of the workplace as a competitive playing field and thinks exclusively in terms of sporting events. Vocal volume is usually high, enthusiasm comes in sudden spurts, and meetings often take on a creepy, huddle-like feeling. Back-slapping and high-fives only contribute to the general feeling of gloom and impending defeat.

>>>*BEST DEFENSE:* Detached amusement makes this boss feel appreciated without feeling threatened. There is no need to soil your soul by playing along and referring to "innings," "fourth-quarters," or "time-outs." Do your work efficiently, but don't get sucked into "the game."

THE SOCCER MOM BOSS

Unable or unwilling to jump into the fray, this boss stands on the sidelines nervously wringing hands and texting concerns to unknown entities on handheld devices. They may be male or female, but the defining factor is an utter inability to take charge and make decisions due to the self-imposed sideline status. Countless e-mails document the "roadblocks," "progress," and "wins" of others, but the passive refusal to interfere and a belief that clapping can actually influence outcome usually results in no progress whatsoever.

>>>*BEST DEFENSE:* Firm decisions and proactive measures dazzle such bosses because when they see progress, they believe that magic is in play. Get anything at all done and they will think you are a golden wizard.

THE OBSESSIVE, BUSY BOSS

DID YOU KNOW?

The tax manual given to IRS employees actually has instructions for collecting taxes after a nuclear war.

Always frenzied and making a show of their importance, this is the boss who is uneasy when things go smoothly. Chaos is expected and smooth, calm efficiency is distrusted. Quantity of work is valued more than quality, so workers are given useless tasks, needless reports are deemed essential, documentation of every bowel movement is required, and all employees end up devoting their time to supporting the swirl created by the busy one.

>>>*BEST DEFENSE:* This boss is easily appeased by numbers and itemized lists. Don't just report that you finished the task. Report that you documented 145 pieces of data, requiring twelve follow up calls, and you've saved a copy of the document on the shared server. They'll eat that shit up.

THE MARTYR BOSS

The beleaguered martyr boss will take on all duties leaving the staff shrugging as they surf the internet. Chances for advancement, however, are limited under such a character, but it does make for a fun atmosphere if your coworkers have a healthy sense of fun and irony. Even so, sudden bursts of resentment can surface, so it doesn't hurt to volunteer occasionally for the easy tasks because, at some point, the martyr will unexpectedly become resentful.

>>>*BEST DEFENSE:* Maintain your responsibilities and make an effort now and then to impress because the rubber band will inevitably snap back at some point and you don't want to be the one caught with your pants down.

THE BOSSHOLE

This would be the truly loathsome individual, consistently insufferable and beyond redemption. He or she may exhibit any number of characteristics from any other of the prototypes, but at their core they are simply small, mean, and evil. An intolerable working atmosphere is sensed by all and the only comfort to be had is the knowledge that this beast will have to spend the rest of his or her life in their own presence.

>>>*BEST DEFENSE:* Walk away. Nothing is worth such misery. But before you do, take a few notes and document a few incriminating facts to make your stop at the HR office on your way out worthwhile.

Additional Tips

Regardless of which type of boss you are reporting to—and bosses may fall into more than one category—there a few good rules of thumb to keep in mind:

▲ Try to establish a good social relationship with your boss's boss. If your immediate boss sees this, he or she will be more likely to speak highly of you and less likely to say anything that might destroy their boss's happy impression.

▲ Find out exactly how much time off you are entitled to and always keep track of your own vacation and sick days in the event that they are called into question.

▲ For the same reason, keep an updated list of every completed project, ongoing duties, and achievements.

▲ Make deadlines and personal accountability your primary concerns. An awful lot of effort is required to redeem oneself after a missed deadline or a botched project, so cover your ass.

▲ Do not trash your coworkers in discussions with the boss. Expressing "concern" is a far more effective way of addressing real issues without setting up conflicts or ill feeling.

▲ Do not kiss up. Though your boss will love having you at their beck and call, it is unlikely that you will be garnering much respect. It's more likely you'll just end up doing extra work.

▲ Make the boss laugh. In any scenario the employee who can reduce tension and inspire a good chuckle is always favored.

Your Cast of Coworkers

Obviously, it pays to play well with others in the workplace. A concerted effort to get along with all of your coworkers can only work to your own benefit in the long run, so regardless of whether you would ever want to know these people outside of the office, as in global politics, it is well worth your time to establish good relations and create alliances with solid defenses in place.

Once again, a true friend in the office is the best-case scenario. Someone who sees the job as you do, shares your sense of humor, and is a trusted ally is the best that you can ask for. But even in the absence of such a character, office relationships can be rewarding and valuable if properly cultivated. Identifying the species in question is the essential starting point for any serious scientific analysis. Who is in your workplace?

THE BITTER LEMON

This would be the disgruntled—though often hilarious—cynic who considers their very presence in the workplace an insult to their innate superiority. Such characters can be good fun if you can connect to their core.

>>> *BEST DEFENSE:* Make friends. Everyone needs to vent now and then, and this is the ideal person to hook up with for savage attacks on superiors and happy-hour reflections on workplace ironies. However, a strong force field is required lest their tendencies toward self-sabotage may creep into your consciousness.

THE POLLYANNA

A goody-two-shoes demeanor is often a hard pill to swallow, and caution is always advisable when dealing with the unnaturally perky. Remember that a sugary façade often masks a vicious nature, so don't be fooled by the sunny disposition.

>>> *BEST DEFENSE:* Due to a penchant for tattling this character is best kept safely appeased with general pleasantries, good will, and mild intimidation. Becoming friends is unnecessary, but a friendly approach coupled with clear boundaries will make it clear that you are not to be trifled with.

THE COMPETITOR

The competitive coworker can often be identified by false charm and a questioning nature. Usually displaying a gregarious nature, this one is out to find your weak spots and undermine your achievements—not necessarily out of malice, but rather due to a deeply ingrained and psychotic need to outdo others and "win."

>>>*BEST DEFENSE:* Refuse to compete. These characters tend to shoot themselves in the foot when given the opportunity. Concentrate on your own responsibilities and never respond when they try to upstage you by drawing attention to their own accomplishments. Chances are their own insecurities will be the shovel with which they dig their own grave.

THE LOSER

While losers come in many forms, the one common characteristic they all share is that they are easily identified. In many cases their hapless hopelessness can seem oddly endearing—and therein lies an excellent opportunity for mentoring.

>>>*BEST DEFENSE:* Protect your own karma by being a decent person. Once out of the third grade there is nothing to be gained by being cruel to the less fortunate, so recognize opportunity when it lumbers awkwardly toward you and be a good person.

THE VICTIM

Paranoid and defensive, this grievous character loves nothing more than being screwed over because their entire self-image has been formed in response to an unfair world in which they have the starring role as the victim. They wait for it, they expect it, and, not surprisingly, they usually get it right between the eyes.

>>> *BEST DEFENSE:* Play the role of the encouraging confidant. It is not your place to disabuse them of their carefully constructed self-image, but by offering occasional encouragement and a sympathetic ear you can win their favor without being sucked into their vortex of negativity.

THE SUCK-UP

There's one in every office and it's never pretty. This is the character you know to be evil and conniving, but who masks their intentions with false enthusiasm and calculated ploys to impress the boss. They invariably volunteer for things, are first in line for the softball team, and eagerly participate whenever mandatory fun is scheduled by the boss.

>>> *BEST DEFENSE:* The resolve and determination of a suck-up is best chipped away at over time. By pretending to be impressed with their work ethic and enthusiasm you will find ample opportunities to nominate them for the crap jobs that no one else would dream of taking: "Well, I think Marjorie would do a stellar job of organizing all the employee birthday celebrations."

THE MANIPULATOR

This could be you, so be careful. The manipulator is often revealed by his or her attempts to weasel out of things and dump responsibilities on others. Always angling for the plum assignments or the preferred pods, they are often betrayed by their own nervous energy.

>>>*BEST DEFENSE:* Strike back early. Characters such as these are always assessing who the most likely candidates might be for their evil plans of dominance. Establish early on through prolonged stares and raised eyebrows that you see through them and that you are not easily deceived. If they're funny, join forces.

Underlings and Subordinates

If, despite the odds, you actually find yourself moving up in the company, your greatest power resides in the way that you deal with your subordinates. Though your instincts may tell you that your boss is the one on whom you should be focused, the employees you manage also play a pivotal role in ensuring your stability and balance on the corporate ladder. From the analyses presented in previous sections of this chapter, it should be quite clear that bullying, excessive control, and intimidation always backfire.

On the flip side, it is never wise to be a pushover who lives in fear of being disliked. You will do much better by establishing clear and reasonable boundaries along with a healthy sense of humor and an atmosphere of trust and respect. But trust is not to be confused with gullibility. If you are in a supervisory position, you must keep your eyes and ears open to ensure that those little rascals aren't screwing you over. Even the most trusted and likeable characters will be tempted to skate by and slack off if the opportunity presents itself. That being the case, a wink and a nod combined with a tight agenda and clearly drawn deadlines is your best approach. Additionally:

▲ Try to avoid asking your employees to do things you yourself would find disagreeable.

▲ If disagreeable tasks are required, acknowledge the fact and explain the necessity.

▲ Give credit where credit is due and seek to advance those who deserve it.

▲ Keep meetings short and discussions light. Resort to gravitas only when necessary.

▲ Remember that humor always lessens the drudgery and makes the workday pass more quickly.

▲ Never allow yourself to become predictable or tedious.

▲ Keep your moods in check and avoid unnecessary drama at all costs.

▲ Buy a round every now and then.

Moving On Up

Now that a few general ground rules have been laid down and a sensible approach to the corporate hierarchy has been established, your work has only just begun. Yes, my friends, there is a lot more to the puzzle than meets the eye, and no stone may be left unturned if you are to become a true master of "The Machine."

CHAPTER

2

Dress Codes and Corporate Clones

"Never wear anything
that panics the cat."
>>> P.J. O'Rourke

The Depths of Perception

WHILE IT'S TRUE THAT PERCEPTION IS subjective and that fashion never signifies anything of great depth, it is also true that we love nothing better than judging others in the workplace. You may think yourself above such things, but you'd be foolish to think that the rest of your twisted and disgruntled coworkers aren't laughing themselves silly over your flood pants, your white ankle boots, or your fur vest. Then again, it might just be that newly frosted hair that has them buzzing. Whatever the case, everyone has an opinion of everyone else, and no one can afford to make a target of him or herself, or risk sending the wrong message.

In most corporate offices it is not uncommon to see an office intern who comes to work in a t-shirt and sneakers while the CEO is usually in a suit. Of course, there are always those CEOs who refuse to acknowledge reality and insist on dressing like a twenty-year-old, but that's a whole different bag of giggles. It's really a simple question of uniform. The way that you dress is an indicator of your status within the company and the way in which you choose to be seen. Generally, those in creative fields have the greatest freedom, but that may also mean greater scrutiny by your fashion-conscious, pursed-lipped, creatively tormented coworkers. Those whose jobs require them to meet with outside clients and partners are generally more restricted, and that means an entirely different kind of scrutiny and attention to detail.

The inescapable fact is that your dress affects the way you are perceived professionally. And while you may feel very pleased with yourself and wildly uncompromised for showing up every day dressed like a Peanuts character, you may actually be damaging your own chances of advancement. By being too casual, you may be sending a message that you are very comfortable with your low-ranking status. This is not to suggest the mailroom clerk will suddenly rocket up the ladder by wearing a suit, but your presentation of yourself is a good indicator to your superiors of how seriously you take your job and your attention to detail. And as such, it is actually one of the easiest ways to manipulate your superiors.

DID YOU KNOW?

According to the Society for Human Resource Management roughly 50 percent of financial, insurance, and real estate companies allow casual dress once a week, but just 34 percent permit it all the time.

Overall, 44 percent of all businesses have adopted all-casual, all-the-time policies.

Fashionipulation

The most important aspect of manipulation through fashion, or "fashionipulation" as we

shall call it, is the ability to change perceptions with subtlety. If everyone in the office dresses casually, you don't want to stand out awkwardly by aiming too high. Also, bear in mind that there is a significant difference between casual and slovenly. By dressing in a casually stylish manner you present a healthy aura of self-awareness and a finger-on-the-pulse, hipster sensibility. On the other hand, if it always looks as if you pulled your outfit out of the laundry bag, you'll just look like a slob. If you work in a more formal atmosphere, you'll need to adhere to the dress code without completely abandoning your sense of style. Formal dress does not have to mean boring. Conversely, you won't be doing yourself any favors wearing cheap, ill-fitting, formal clothes with the excuse that you have no choice in the matter. You always have a choice. You need to choose a uniform that expresses both your individuality and creative flair without going off the rails.

We've all seen the telemagazine shows that prove how the more attractive applicant always gets the job, but attractiveness is always in the eye of the beholder, and nothing is more attractive than a person who is both unique and has a strong sense of self. By far the most fatal error you can commit is to be bland, devolve into an invisible corporate clone, and disappear into the woodwork. It's a tricky balance, but luckily there are simple guidelines. Whether you work in a chic, high-powered corporation or you are struggling to assert your style beneath some hideous smock you are forced to wear, the same rules apply:

▲ Never wear anything that is wrinkled or rumpled. It indicates sloppiness and that is never a positive attribute in the workplace.

▲ Always dress as fashionably as your budget will allow. If you do it well, people will be more likely to trust in your creative ideas.

▲ Choose clothes that flatter your best assets. Un-PC though it may be, it never hurts to be sexually appealing to anyone who might notice, but subtlety is essential.

▲ At all costs you must avoid looking trashy. This is the ultimate fashion failure. You may get laid at the holiday party but you'll never get respect.

▲ Always dress appropriately for the position above your own. The people who get promoted are those who look as though they fit the bill.

▲ Maintain your individuality. Do not cave in and opt for a corporate generic uniform or you will fade completely out of sight and become part of the furniture.

▲ Invest what you can in your workplace wardrobe. People are easily swayed and good shoes are always a good investment.

"Clothes make the man. Naked people have little or no influence on society."
>>> Mark Twain

Are you thinking that this is all very superficial, and it's really the work you do that counts? Well, you are partially correct. It is superficial and no one gets promoted on the basis of their wardrobe. However, there is simply no denying that visual imagery plays a significant part in the ways in which we evaluate, assess, and yes, judge others. You can rage against the machine in your polyester pantsuit, or you can put in a little time and thought, make the most of what you've got, and reap the benefits. It is entirely up to you.

Crimes and Misdemeanors

Perhaps, at this juncture, a brief review of taboos would be a good way to establish some parameters. As previously mentioned there are certain faux pas that will surely guarantee a slow slide into invisibility. These are to be avoided at all costs. The corporate workplace is a treacherous and insidious arena that can sap the individuality right out of a person, leaving behind little more than a poorly dressed, hopeless cog in the grand wheel.

In the age of the metrosexual and the office power minx, the competition is definitely fierce. If you allow yourself to become a corporate clone—

with all its dreary implications—you will not only be jeopardizing your own advancement up the ladder, but you will also be joining the ranks of the anonymous and the defeated. Truly, if you think about it, by abandoning your true self and all that that entails, you are in effect throwing in the towel and proclaiming yourself "average." And the average never achieve the extraordinary.

So, what are these precarious taboos, you ask? What choices are most likely to render you invisible? Let us review:

FOR MEN

Pleated Khakis: The "Jiffy-Pop" effect fools no one and the silhouette of a pear does not inspire confidence.

Company Logo Shirts: Unless required, they simply announce that you have absolutely no sense of yourself outside of work.

Denim Shirts: Not laid-back, not sexy, not youthful—just bland.

Amorphous Shoes: Nothing says "schlub" like a bad pair of shoes.

Christmas Sweaters: Neither cute nor charming—just sad.

Hawaiian Shirts: Not on casual Friday, not at the company picnic, not ever.

Colorful Vests: One of the few garments in the world that can age you by a full decade.

Skinny Ponytail with Earring: It doesn't say rebel, it says overgrown geek with a taste for air-guitar.

FOR WOMEN

A Style-Free, Bob Haircut: A stylish bob is one thing, but hanging hair-curtains do not tend to flatter.

A Short String of Pearls: Two words: Barbara Bush.

Fair-Isle Sweaters with a Wool Skirt: Yeah, yeah, you're preppy, we get it. We don't care where you grew up.

Tight, Stretchy Pants: It is always unwise to advertise the fact that you need "stretch."

Leggings: Unless you can turn back time, there is no excuse.

Panty Hose: Hi, Grandma!

Sneakers with a Skirt Suit: Better to be wildly uncomfortable than to ever be seen this way.

Berets: You may be thinking Parisian beatnik, but everyone else is thinking Monica Lewinsky.

Leather and Lace: Stevie Nicks barely got away with it. You shouldn't even think about it.

Beyond the Pale

"Know, first, who you are; and then adorn yourself accordingly."
>>> Epictetus

Though it is very important not to disappear, it is far more important not to be disgusting. In a class of their own, there are a few surefire faux pas for both men and women that will virtually guarantee a total lack of respect in the office:

THE WHALE TAIL: This would be the visible thong or G-string hovering above the waistband of your "sexy" jeans!

THE MUFFIN TOP: A 360-degree protrusion of fat spilling over the too-tight waistband of your supposedly alluring low-rider pants. Not so alluring after all.

THE SAUSAGE TOP: A hideously tight top (especially in Spandex) that draws unwanted attention to a woman's back fat or a man's beer boobs.

THE "CHARACTER" HAT: Any hat featuring fur, unreasonable altitude, or feathers will only elicit sad glances and resigned chuckles from your coworkers.

PICKLE STABBERS: Boots or shoes with frighteningly high, narrow, and sharp heels. Save your dominatrix gear for the weekends.

PULLUNDER: A stretchy unitard-like item worn beneath an oversized sweater or smock-like garment. Only acceptable in speed-skating or pantomime class.

THE TRANSWESTITE: This would be the urban male who insists on dressing in cowboy regalia. There is no justifiable reason for this.

THE SEASONONO: Lightweight linens, cotton suits, or Easter Egg colors in winter will only make you look confused and possibly crazy. It's no different than wearing a turtleneck in July.

UNNECESSARILY COMPLICATED JEANS: Weird zippers, multiple side-pockets, exposed button-flys, shreddy patches, and snaps are all risky business on their own. In excessive combination they are laughable.

EXTREME IRONING: Your jeans and your t-shirts are not meant to have creases. Try to keep your unnatural compulsions in check.

GOING COMMANDO: There is so little to be gained by going without underwear when so very much can go wrong.

If you ever find yourself standing in front of a mirror, asking yourself if something looks stupid, it probably does. At the very least, you are not comfortable in it or else you wouldn't be asking the question. A simple rule of thumb when in doubt is to keep it simple and follow common sense:

▲ Wear clothes that fit you properly.

▲ Remember that dark colored items can be worn more often.

▲ Avoid costumes.

▲ Dry clean the good stuff.

▲ Keep loud colors and patterns to a minimum.

▲ Know that wild styles become quickly outdated.

▲ Don't forget the 'do.

▲ Keep the nose hairs in check.

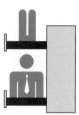

Making the Most of Casual Fridays

If your office is among those with strict dress codes, "Casual Friday" may be your one weekly chance to surprise people. It's not an excuse to look dumpy, but rather it's your chance to exert sex appeal! Of course, you may want to stop short of stepping out of the elevator in a cupcake thong and a top hat, but there are some good options for the shrewd employee who is able to recognize opportunity:

❖ **Wear your most flattering jeans:** If allowed— and if they actually look good—you can present your ass in a whole new light.

❖ **Trot out your best shoes:** Try not to go overboard, but an excellent pair of shoes can be very eye-catching and may surprise coworkers who have underestimated the contents of your character and your closet.

❖ **Employ your nicely fitted top:** This does not mean stretchy. Lycra and Spandex are always a mistake, but a nicely tapered shirt or blouse can effectively highlight your efforts at the gym and raise eyebrows in a good way.

❖ **Try out your stylish vintage item:** Extremes are to be avoided, but a good character piece on a youthful employee can be a nice reminder that you do have a sense of style and a life beyond the office. Of course, after a certain age vintage clothing simply reads as old and outdated.

❖ **Go for Quality Casual:** Take the opportunity to go casual without drifting into sloppiness by wearing quality, elegant items. A cool jacket with a loose tie, a relaxed, stylish dress, or any combination of good designer clothes will send the message that, try as you might, you just can't look dumpy.

Shortcuts When You're Running Late

Obviously, none of us can manage to look fantastic all the time, especially after a big night out or on those days when you just don't have the energy. On those stressful mornings when you find yourself running late, there a few quick shortcuts that can be employed to get you out the door a little quicker without completely compromising your appearance:

A Stylish Stubble: Don't have enough time to shave? Just clean up the edges and play it off as sexy.

The Sleek Ponytail: Can't be bothered with the full production? Pull it tight and get an instant facelift too.

The All-Black Ensemble: The perfect choice on laundry day or on those mornings when the snooze alarm fails.

Bed-Head Chic: Disguise a bad hair day with a great outfit. Let them think it's intentional.

Sporty Style: If you're really late, go for a casual, athletically themed ensemble with comfortable shoes in which you can run.

Visine and an Ice-Water Splash: The absolute minimum to create an illusion of alertness.

The Emergency Desk Drawer

Regardless of how much effort you put into personal grooming or fashion at work, every employee should have a drawer properly stocked for hygiene emergencies. Of course, all personal grooming should always be done with the greatest discretion, so a trip to the bathroom is probably best, but being prepared for the unexpected is simply common sense. The following desk-drawer checklist of must-haves may save you from a variety of humiliating scenarios:

Tissues: Nothing will ruin your credibility faster than a nasal floater.

Tweezers: Wild nose hairs or crazy ear hairs often appear without warning.

Nail Clippers: Not for clipping but for emergency hangnails and the like.

Dental Floss: Essential to combat the perils of poppy seed muffins and other dangers.

Eye Drops: Always useful for tired eyes, allergies, dry eyes, or hangovers.

Deodorant: For unusually hot summer days and those rare times you forget at home.

Mints: Always a good idea before important meetings and after a stinky lunch.

Q-Tips: There is little in life more disconcerting than a dislodged wax ball.

A Hand Mirror: Only for the quick fixes—major repairs should be conducted in the privacy of a bathroom stall.

PLEASE
RE-GROOM

Employee Expansion

Understanding the importance of uniform and personal grooming in the workplace is important, but there are other considerations to take into account that affect not only your self-esteem, but also your health and general well-being.

Have you gained weight since you were hired? Has your waistline been increasing and your confidence decreasing in direct proportion to your years of employment? Are your eyes slowly crossing as your ass is slowly widening? Well, you are not alone. The security of a "stable job" with benefits tends to subconsciously convince us that leaving the office for any reason will be perceived as a problem. You actually went to lunch at a restaurant? Why would you go for a walk? Is there a problem? Are you plotting an escape from the compound? Why all this crazy self-indulgence?

The sad fact is that most corporate employees live in perpetual fear of appearing anything less than 100 percent committed to the workplace. Even though an hour-long lunch is considered standard, most corporate employees are terrified of actually devoting a full hour to lunch. Instead, they hurry to the nearest fast food joint and rush back to their pods to fortify themselves while simultaneously reading e-mails and running reports. Others will produce sad little Tupperware coffins from home that are filled with celery or last night's dreary pasta.

Ironically, these people are digging themselves into a hole. If you are always online, you will be identified as the go-to person who is always available and you will find yourself at the bottom of a perpetual pile of delegated duties. You must recognize that your lazy superiors are always monitoring your availability as they probably have an infinite supply of work to dump on you.

By confidently committing to your "away" time you can send a subtle though effective message that you are not the one upon whom shit may be dumped. If you are at lunch, you are at lunch. How you use that lunch time is up to you. Do not cave in to the insidious temptation to drown your frustrations in comfort food.

Considerations of health care costs aside, nothing pleases a corporate employer more than an increasingly expanding employee with their self-esteem on the downswing. You think those Krispy Kreme donuts in the kitchen are an act of generosity on the part of your employer? They are not. They are part of an evil plot to accommodate your most base instincts while simultaneously producing a sugar high and undermining your confidence. Think about it. Are glazed donuts really the reward you were looking for?

But beyond the kitchen temptations and wildly fatty treats that your employer offers, your own personal eating habits are yours to monitor. Extreme vigilance is required lest you slide into a state of passive complacency. After all, you'll need to be fit to run around town looking for that new job when the pink slips suddenly start raining down.

Quick Tips for Expanding Employees

If your waistline is increasing faster than your income, try a few of these ideas to ensure your own personal downsizing:

▲ Avoid the vending machines: Evil often comes in small plastic bags.

▲ Take the stairs instead of the elevator: Small steps can yield big results.

▲ Always keep drinking water on hand: The more you drink the more it fills you up.

▲ Pass on the homemade cookies your coworker made: Avoid the sugar crash.

▲ Get up and move on your lunch hour: Fend off that flat ass.

▲ Communicate in person: Don't e-mail your every thought. Move around and talk to people.

▲ Get off the subway at an earlier stop: Extend your walking time.

▲ Don't drive or take a cab if you can walk: This applies to weekends as well.

▲ Park on the top floor of the parking structure: The extra stair climbing adds up.

These, of course, are the baby steps for the chronically lazy. If going to the gym, practicing yoga, or training for marathons are more your speed, then all the more power to you. Not only will you be taking control of your own health and well-being, but the accumulated time you will be spending on yourself is that much less time spent worrying and tormenting yourself about the job.

Yes, it's obvious, but it's also very easy to become complacent. And when you become complacent, you lose energy, ambition, and focus. Over time the pressures of a job, whether it's highly demanding or painfully boring, can slowly begin to sap away our passions, our enthusiasm, and our enjoyment of our lives. So, whether it's strenuous exercise or something as simple as a long walk through the park, make sure you keep moving. After all, sitting in a pod and typing don't really burn very many calories.

DID YOU KNOW?

THE BULGE REPORT

According to CareerBuilder.com's "Work and Health 2005" survey, 47 percent of workers report that they have gained weight since they began work at their current jobs.

CHAPTER

3

Pod
Culture

"Computers are useless.
They can only
give you answers."
>>> Pablo Picasso

The Rise of Cubism

IT WAS ONCE A TERM ASSOCIATED WITH avant-garde art in an age when the deconstruction of traditions was embraced by some and reviled by others. It was new and modern, and it was therefore exciting. But that was a different time. And in an increasingly corporate world, there is little room for exciting, radical, new ideas. It's all about profit now, and that is why you don't have your own office.

There was a time in the corporate world when a person who rose to any midlevel position would be given a private office in which to conduct business. Doors could be closed to ensure privacy, and usually a secretary would be situated outside of the office to screen and announce visitors and phone calls. And in these days of old, a three-martini lunch was considered commonplace. I know, it all sounds crazy and impossible, but it truly was so.

In the modern workplace a private office is reserved for the privileged few. For most, the workday consists of sitting in a small, gray cubicle that is void of character and indistinguishable from the countless others that surround it. Well, they used to be called cubicles, but in a world of ever-diminishing attention spans, that's just too many syllables. Now they are known as "pods."

In some cases we have become so accustomed, so accepting of our pod culture that those with low walls actually envy those with an added partition creating a higher wall. The very notion of privacy is not even a question anymore as neighbors and passersby can easily listen in on your phone calls, eavesdrop on your conversations, or see what is displayed on your computer screen at any time.

Of course, the lack of personal privacy also means that we are regularly and unmercifully subjected to the personal phone calls and inane conversations of those who have been plunked nearby. In the average workplace the odds of being completely surrounded by people you like are very slim indeed. Invariably, there will be someone within earshot who is loud, void of personal boundaries, and probably has an excruciatingly annoying laugh. This phenomenon is most likely the single most effective driving force of headphone sales.

Blame It on Bob

So, your work life is confined to a small gray pod with little more than a computer, a phone, and a filing

DID YOU KNOW?

The production of office cubicles accounts for the largest share of office furniture sales in the world, with profits estimated in the area of $3 billion each year.

DID YOU KNOW?

In an effort to reduce spending the U.S. Securities and Exchange Commission, the Department of Justice, and the State Department are required by law to offer eligible employees the option of telecommuting or working from home.

cabinet? Is your ability to control the atmosphere of your workspace limited to the rearranging of colorful magnets? Is this what you had in mind during all those years of schooling, while you were taking out all those student loans and dreaming of your fantastic career? Probably not.

Life in a pod is not what most of us aspire to, but sadly, the dreaded "pod farm" has become commonplace in a variety of industries as an inexpensive and easily customized means of cramming the maximum number of employees into the minimum amount of space. Most would agree that it is a rather soul-crushing arrangement to say the least. So, who's the asshole who thought this up, you ask? Please allow me now to draw your attention to one Bob Propst—the inventor of the office cubicle.

Now to be fair, Mr. Propst agrees that the modern interpretation of his once-groundbreaking invention has indeed become something of a monstrosity. When he was approached in the early 1960s by D. J. Dupree, founder of the Herman Miller Company, he had been inventing solutions for a wide range of companies and his work included the development of new ways to produce concrete as well as improved seating for pilots of supersonic jets. Dupree invited Propst to try his hand at furniture design in an effort to provide alternatives to the standard rows of clunky desks with shared filing cabinets in distant locations that contained an infinite number of shared files.

His vision was one of happy employees moving about and interacting freely while gloriously modern, semi-enclosed spaces afforded limited privacy. Further, by equipping each cubicle with its own filing cabinets and shelving, employees would be able to manage their own paperwork and filing more efficiently. Ironically, his original goal was to get away from boxes and corridors and, by providing tackboards and display surfaces, he was trying to provide an opportunity for employees to "individualize" their spaces and create a more personalized atmosphere.

Of course, as mass production began, cheaper materials were used, the size of the pods shrunk exponentially, and the boxes and corridors were back. In an interview with *Metropolis* magazine in 1998 Propst said: "The dark side of this is that not all organizations are intelligent and progressive. Lots are run by crass people who can take the same kind of equipment and create hellholes. They make little bitty cubicles and stuff people into them. Barren, rat-hole places." Indeed.

So, maybe Bob doesn't really deserve our collective scorn. He tried. And if it's gonna be pods, it's gonna be pods, so there's little point in trying to undo what has been done. Instead,

DID YOU KNOW?

Research has shown that the most productive workday is Tuesday and the least productive is Friday.

the creative captive employee of the twenty-first century will make the most of the situation, master the subtleties of pod culture, and defy the oppressive atmosphere in a variety of ways.

POD-FREE

Looking to escape that dreary cubicle? Consider these fields of employment that are most conducive to working from home:

❖ Sales Reps

❖ Consultants

❖ Financial Types

❖ Lawyers

❖ Writers

❖ Graphic Artists

❖ Researchers

Pod Décor

An oxymoron, you say? Perhaps, but given the amount of time that you sit in that little cube of yours, it's worth at least making an effort to improve things. Happily, there are a few creative tricks that can be employed, though there are also a few pitfalls to avoid. Let us first address the list of unforgivable pod crimes that will only lessen your popularity in the workplace and slowly erode your fragile sense of self:

BAD IDEAS:

Figurines: Your obsession with Star Trek, Lord of the Rings, or Bobble Heads is a shameful, embarrassing secret that should be kept hidden at all costs, not displayed.

Stuffed Animals: Unless you wish to be known as a sexless, insecure, and baby-like employee, do not display your teddies, bunnies, or suction-cup Garfields.

Company Swag: The occasional free coffee mug is one thing, but a plethora of logo-ridden, useless knick knacks from the company store signifies a complete lack of dignity and individuality.

Excessive Displays of Photos: A few photos of loved ones is fine, but a wall-eclipsing collage with photos of everyone you've ever known is a huge yawn to those around you.

Silly Pens and Pencils: Despite what they may say, no one is really amused by your kooky troll pencil or your hilarious giant crayon display. Get rid of them.

Balloons: If you have someone in your life that actually sends you balloons at work, for whatever reason, do not display them any longer than is necessary. Immediately call the person who who sent them and ask them never to do so again.

Calendars with Kittens: The associated imagery of lace doilies, sickening perfume, colonial furniture, and floral bedspreads is simply too much to ask your coworkers to bear.

College Paraphernalia: If you have graduated, it's over. You don't need to advertise your belief that your best years are behind you.

Excessive Sports Memorabilia: If you're a serious fan, an item or two is perfectly acceptable. Anything more than that just makes you look twice as sad sitting there in your nonathletic pod.

Piles of Trash: If you are a slob at home, at least try to conceal that fact at work. Piles of useless paper, fast food bags, newspapers, and assorted junk will only create the impression of insanity.

On the other side of the coin, let us review a few ideas that may actually improve that dreary little space in which you toil:

GOOD IDEAS:

Photos of Your Travels: These can be inspirational reminders of why you work in the first place. Whether they are places you have been or places you intend to go, they remind you of your true life.

A Table Lamp: Soft lighting is more relaxing, less stressful to the eye, and far more flattering for anyone over thirty. Bring in a lamp and then climb up on your desk and unscrew that hideous neon thing above you.

A Plant or Two: If only to remind you that there is still life on Earth, a hard-to-kill plant can provide a tenuous connection to the natural world.

A Sensible Calendar: No airbrushed monster cars, no sci-fi fantasies, no Hooters' girls, and no babies sitting in watermelon rinds. A simple tasteful photographic calendar from a museum or your travels is a far superior and more dignified choice.

Touches of Humor: An ironic sign, a smart cartoon, or a humorous trinket or two are perfectly reasonable indicators of your sense of humor. Bear in mind that less is more, so choose wisely in order to express your true sentiments.

A Rearview Mirror: No computer screen should be without a clip-on rearview mirror. In order to get ahead you must know who's behind you at all times.

Clean Surfaces: An organized workspace is indicative of an organized mind.

Fun Tricks to Play on Your Neighbors

Though sitting in a pod, day in and day out, can be soul-crushing at best, it is entirely possible to brighten one's day by messing with your neighbor's head. Creative cruelty should be restricted to only the most extreme of circumstances, but a harmless little prank here and there works well on both friends and foes alike. Consider these suggestions for needling your neighbors:

▲ Tell the new girl the office copier is voice-activated.

▲ Tell the new guy that the first Tuesday of every month is Cross Dressing Day.

▲ Select one of her figurines and move it to a new position every day.

▲ While he's away turn up his computer speakers to full volume.

▲ Leave a hideously sappy greeting card in her pod and sign it "You Know Who."

▲ Disturb his confidence by anonymously leaving an air freshener on his desk.

▲ Leave a Post-It note on her computer screen that says "I know what you did."

▲ Completely readjust his fancy ergonomic chair.

▲ Empty her stapler on a daily basis.

▲ Regularly remove the tape from his tape dispenser and replace it upside down.

▲ Unplug her cute little office lamp.

▲ Place a piece of tape over the mouse ball on his computer mouse.

Curious Subspecies of the Pod Farm

In every office, regardless of size or business, there are certain stock characters who inevitably surface. Though largely harmless, these peculiar species tend to run in packs. Make sure you are not one of them:

THE FREEGAN: A lover of free food. This is the person who rushes excitedly through the office alerting everyone that there are free donuts or leftover sandwiches in the kitchen!

THE WALL HUMPER: That person who is too lazy to remove their ID card from their pocket and ends up thigh-humping the security scanner on the wall.

THE MULTISLACKER: A coworker who is usually on the phone, playing online Sudoku, and reading the tabloids every time you pass their cube.

THE SOCIAL WET TOWEL: This would be the un-invited person who regularly appears from nowhere, drapes himself over the cubicle wall and pointlessly asks "How's it goin'?"

THE POSTAL PROBABILITY: The person in the office most likely to snap can most easily be identified by sullen silences, awkward comments, and a wardrobe consisting primarily of black and olive.

THE CACKLING PARROT: In every office there is someone with a blood-curdling laugh who virtually lives on the phone and is prone to shrieking in delight at the slightest provocation. Best solution: blow darts.

THE SQUATTER: They have a cubicle in your area, they never introduce themselves, and no one in the office has any clue who they work for or why they are there. Interestingly, this character will likely outlast everyone else on the floor.

THE CONFERASSHOLE: Unable or unwilling to don a headset or actually pick up the phone, this idiot places every caller on speakerphone, forcing everyone in earshot to suffer through their tedious business.

The Walls Have Eyes

Now, hopefully, as a savvy citizen of the twenty-first century you are not laboring under the delusion that you have any real privacy in the workplace just because no one is looking. Of course, you're not. You couldn't possibly be that naïve. I'm sure you're perfectly aware that, as the American Management Association points out, approximately 78 percent of U.S. companies use some method of tracking their employees' work behavior, communications, and messaging. These techniques most commonly include:

❖ Monitoring your e-mails.

❖ Tracking your instant messages.

❖ Monitoring your use of software, systems, or programs.

❖ Checking logs of your phone calls.

❖ Listening in on your phone calls.

❖ Conducting video surveillance.

❖ Tracking the websites you visit.

❖ Having other employees "observe" your behavior.

❖ Eavesdropping on personal conversations.

The truth is "workplace surveillance" (or, to you and me, spying) is a lot more pervasive than most employees realize. In recent years companies such as Websense, SurfControl, and Secure Computing have seen their profits soar as they have developed software that allows employers to track your every keystroke, e-mail, instant message, or phone call. Oh, yes, my little friends, Big Brother has got your number.

In theory the justification for such spying is that employers need to protect themselves from theft, the leaking of company secrets, or the involvement in illegal activities by its employees. So, chances are that, unless you're plotting to overthrow The Man or are leaking secrets to the competition, you shouldn't get entirely paranoid just yet. However, it is important to remember that employers are most likely to track your activities if you are using company-owned computers or phone systems. Now, while an occasional surf through your favorite weblogs or sports sites shouldn't result in a pink slip, the general rule of thumb is that you should never send any questionable communications or visit any incriminating websites on your work computer.

In the event that you have a truly evil boss who you believe might frown upon your insider trading, your pornography obsession, or your little habit of visiting terrorist chat rooms, it would behoove you to do that shit at home on your own laptop. And don't kid yourself that any primitive attempts to clear your cache or erase your history of websites visited will protect you. Your company wouldn't spend big money on a system that is that easily fooled. Trust that every little item you input is being stored somewhere. If at any point you are having difficulty deciding on the ethics of a given situation, just imagine yourself in court, having a jury—along with your family in the front row—being treated to a review of your behaviors in question. That should do it.

Of course, laws and protective measures are being bandied about to protect workers, but in legal contests courts have generally ruled in favor of employers, citing that they have the right to monitor activities on equipment that they own. However, if an employee has a personal e-mail account that they access through a workplace computer, the employer cannot access that activity using the employee's computer and password. In any case such legal technicalities

DID YOU KNOW?

According to a survey by ePolicy-AMA:

60 percent of U.S. companies currently use software to monitor both incoming and outgoing external e-mail.

27 percent of employers admit to using software that tracks internal e-mail between employees.

10 percent of companies have taken steps to enable them to monitor desktop chat.

rarely come into play until long after you have been accused of corporate treachery, and at that point it's all about the lawyers.

Just watch your back, keep an eye out for the hidden cameras, and keep smiling.

Tips to Foil the Spies

Given that an ever-increasing number of companies are embracing the idea of spying on employees, you can minimize your risk by keeping a few practical ideas in mind:

▲ Read up on the company's rules and regulations to learn what is and is not allowed in your particular workplace.

▲ Step outside with a cell phone for any personal calls you don't want your neighbors listening in on.

▲ Avoid visiting any questionable websites at work. Not only could your computer use be monitored, anyone could walk up and see what you're doing at any time.

▲ Be aware of your arrival and departure times. The daily swipes you make with that little security badge are most likely being logged in at some database to track your comings and goings.

▲ Turn off your computer when you are away from your desk, unless you don't mind that evil coworker popping by and reading your e-mails.

▲ Remember that every e-mail you send from your work account may be forwarded to anyone else at any time.

▲ Don't use the company credit card for any questionable personal purchases.

It seems as if the twenty-first century has taken all the fun out of deviant pleasures. We are all on display, we are all being videotaped, and someone, somewhere, in some distant basement is watching everything that's happening on our computer screens. The days of reckless abandon have passed. You can't even kill someone anymore without having your breath particles retrieved from the atmosphere. It's really very sad.

But once again, adaptation is the key to survival. Do not fear that strange little glass bulb protruding from the ceiling that occasionally whirrs and blinks a red light in your direction. Wave hello, and let the monitoring minions know that you enjoy their admiring eyes. Don't be self-conscious about having sex in the copy room—just be sure to turn the lights out. And above all do not let those three-and-one-half gray walls pin you in or squash your spirit.

The Cleaning Crew

Isn't it nice how the cleaning crew shows up each evening and tidies up after you? Aren't they a selfless bunch, working so tirelessly and seemingly invisible all the while? It's really quite marvelous isn't it? Well, maybe not. Before you sink into a warm and fuzzy state of admiration, keep in mind that the cleaning crew is just as bitter, bored, and devious as you are, if not more so. Just take a moment and think about how your own carelessness may be revealing more about you than you might like to think.

Again, don't leave your computer on overnight: Are you condescendingly assuming that the cleaning crew doesn't know how to open up your files and have themselves a good ol' chuckle over your personal e-mails, your history of visited websites, and your spreadsheet ranking the office hotties?

Watch the trash: Nothing reveals our true nature more than the disgusting things we throw away. Your personal to-do lists, dental floss, multiple snack bags, nasty tissues, credit card statements, and flyers from escort services may be painting a very colorful picture of you.

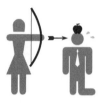

Lock your drawers: Do you really want someone rifling through your secret list of passwords, your personal hygiene items, or your secret stash?

Don't pee when they're cleaning: Avoid supreme awkwardness when the crew is cleaning the bathrooms. Defecating in a freshly cleaned toilet, splashing water all over a wiped down surface, or tossing a crumpled hand towel in a fresh garbage liner is simply bad form. Back out humbly and return to do your nasty business once they're gone.

Don't leave food in the kitchen overnight: Ever since the days of ancient Rome, tampering with food has always been the easiest way to exact revenge on the insensitive or the resented. As the emperor's wife once said to a favored guest: "If I were you I would avoid the pears."

As always, it pays to treat all coworkers with respect, courtesy, and a healthy touch of paranoia. You just never know.

CHAPTER

4

The Art
of Office
Politics

"The secret of success
is sincerity.
Once you can fake that
you've got it made."
>>> Jean Giraudoux

Procedures and Politics

IN EVERY OFFICE THERE ARE POLITICS.
Anyone who has ever joined a new company
quickly learns that there is a Jungian collective
unconscious effect in play that dictates how
things are and are not done. So, before a new
worker can effect any changes whatsoever, he
or she must first understand the existing rules
of the game. Some corporations invest heavily
in regimented training of a militaristic nature
that leaves no questions unanswered. In others
new employees are simply tossed into the deep
end of the pool and expected to figure things
out for themselves. In either case the first order
of business is to understand the processes and
practices of a given company.

Does everything in your office happen on the
fly? Is it bogged down in an endless series of
predetermined procedures? Are they big on
documentation or do they just want the job
to get done? These questions will help you
determine the best ways to navigate the tangled
jungle that is your workplace. Consider the
following scenarios:

THE FORM-DRIVEN WORKPLACE

This is a highly regimented office society in which a high premium is placed on following procedure. Nothing is accomplished without the proper forms or paperwork being submitted. This model is typical of government agencies.

UPSIDE: You can always cover your ass by following the rules.

DOWNSIDE: Change is unheard of, productivity is slow, and creativity is usually squashed.

THE UNSTRUCTURED, CREATIVE FREE-FOR-ALL

Such offices usually revolve around a central creative character prone to fits and tantrums, where productivity and efficiency are measured inconsistently and erratically, and promotion or advancement depend more upon prevailing moods than true performance. This model is most commonplace in the music and fashion industries.

UPSIDE: Grand theatrics and emotional meltdowns can be entertaining and fend off boredom.

DOWNSIDE: High stress levels and inconsistency can jangle the nerves and result in increased alcoholism and smoking.

THE GENTEEL DINOSAUR RELIC

Archaic institutions such as these tend to have an unusually elderly workforce and place great emphasis on protocol, procedure, and political niceties. Technological advances are met with suspiciously arched eyebrows and change is never ushered in without painstaking consideration. Political institutions, law firms, and organizations that deal with the arts often fall into this category.

UPSIDE: A relatively calm atmosphere usually prevails and you can remain the "young one" forever.

DOWNSIDE: Over time employees often find their energy levels drop, their senses of humor diminish, and their fashion sense completely evaporates.

THE OBEDIENT ZOMBIE COMPANY

A wide variety of companies share a spooky desire to create a Stepford-like workforce. Employees in such corporations are barraged with propaganda and mind-numbing messages about how fantastically lucky they are to be part of such a stellar organization, and upper-level management usually displays grotesque, cheerleader-like qualities.

UPSIDE: It's fairly easy to fake enthusiasm, and you'll likely find good friends to bond with who share your skepticism.

DOWNSIDE: Occasionally the brain-washing really does work, and a lazy mind can be tricked into complacent submission.

THE COG AND WHEEL MODEL

In exceptionally large corporations or factory settings roles may be clearly defined and repetitive daily duties are the norm. Workers are in place to perform a set function and are rarely expected to contribute any creative ideas or perform any tasks outside of their assigned roles. While this may appeal to youthful slackers and lazy elders it is generally considered the least satisfying working scenario.

UPSIDE: If you do what you are supposed to do, problems and dramas are kept to a minimum.

DOWNSIDE: To realize that you are nothing more than an expendable machine tends not to inspire great enthusiasm, and it can take a lifetime to make any professional headway.

THE EVIL EMPIRE

Though there may be many players involved, true evil tends to trickle down from the top. Organizations headed by a tyrannical, maniacal, and power-crazed CEO usually make for a very toxic work environment. When greed and corruption are the driving forces behind a corporation's every action, the employees suffer

Eject
Me

by association. While some employees who are similarly disposed may buy into the mindset, most are left with an uncomfortable and sometimes indefinable daily feeling of dread and unease.

UPSIDE: You'll get a front-row seat to see evil at work, and you'll get a very clear picture of what you don't want in your next job.

DOWNSIDE: You may be contributing to a larger force that is perpetuating a culture of greed, destruction, or injustice. Don't stay any longer than you have to.

The models listed above are but a few of the potential scenarios in which you may find yourself. But in any case you must ask yourself a few questions: Do you believe in what the company is producing? Is it of value to society? Are you embarrassed to tell people who you work for? Or do you feel good about being a part of it all? This is not to suggest that you must choose between gung-ho enthusiasm or flat-out contempt for the company. On the contrary, most employees feel fairly ambivalent about the overall picture, and that's fine as long as the job is serving its purpose for you. Only if you find yourself in direct conflict with the practices or purposes of the company do you need to truly consider moving on before things really get to you.

In all other situations, at least for the time being, it's all about understanding your place in the larger picture and focusing on your own little piece of the puzzle. After all, that is where you live, and that is where you can gain control of your everyday work experience.

Perception vs. Reality

Truth be told, it is more important to have your superiors perceive you as a stellar employee than it is to actually be a stellar employee. Now, you may choose to go above and beyond the call at all times, you may choose to do only that which is required of you, or you may fall comfortably in the middle of these extremes. But in either case you must execute. Whatever work you do you must do it in a timely, accurate, and efficient manner. That is what will impress your bosses.

There are those who take the phrase "hard work" literally. These people believe that nothing of value is achieved without great struggle, heroic sacrifice, or difficulty in general. In order to justify this misguided belief they always do more than is necessary, they complicate the process, and they drive themselves to the brink of collapse in every endeavor. These people are stupid.

"Hard work
never killed
anybody, but
why take a
chance?"
>>> Edgar
Bergen

Success is the result of focus, prioritization, and organization. If the work is "hard," you are probably not doing it in the best and most efficient manner. If you are overwhelmed and unable to focus, you should probably take a step back and reprioritize. "Good work" is far better than "hard work."

Now for those who would point to Olympic athletes as an example of "hard work" paying off, it should be pointed out that training "smart" is infinitely better than training to the point of exhaustion. No one reaches the top by making things difficult for themselves. The most effective athletic training is geared toward finding the most efficient ways to achieve maximum perfection without expending unnecessary energy. By its very nature, athletic training can be hard, but you won't find any Olympic gold medalists telling you they got to the podium by complicating simple procedures, overwhelming themselves with irrelevant details, or depriving themselves of sleep by redoing that which has already been done.

Essential Diplomacy

One of the most important skills any office worker can possess is an innate sense of diplomacy. It is far more important than talent, vision, enthusiasm, or ruthlessness. Whether you are managing up or managing down (and you should always realize that you are managing everyone), a tactful approach always pays off in the long run. In the larger picture diplomacy is the key to smooth professional sailing, and while it may come naturally to some, it can also be learned.

The ability to skillfully handle interactions, negotiations, disagreements, and even confrontations without arousing hostility is a highly prized quality in an employee. If you are able to be the voice of reason in the midst of chaos and confusion, then you are perceived to be a person who can get things done. If you can help others reach agreements when opinions differ, you will be perceived as a peacemaker. And if you can manage to calm down the boss when he or she is panicking, well, then you become indispensable. And indispensable employees usually get the best assignments. The rules are simple:

❖ Never take anything personally.

❖ Never take sides.

❖ Ask questions rather than making broad statements.

❖ Always acknowledge both sides of a disagreement.

❖ Keep track of each point of agreement during a discussion.

- ❖ Speak separately with individuals involved in a debate to find common ground.

- ❖ Assure all individuals involved that their points are being heard.

- ❖ Acknowledge the positive aspects of a bad idea before you rip it to shreds.

- ❖ At all times, remain calm.

Emotional Intelligence

Upon closer examination it quickly becomes apparent that diplomatic skills are often a sign of emotional intelligence—a concept now regularly assessed in employee interviews and personality tests. An Ivy League degree means very little if the person in possession of it is an emotional basket case. The ability to think clearly in stressful situations, to control your emotions, and to separate your work from your ego are all signs of a high degree of emotional intelligence, while a low degree of emotional intelligence is often evidenced by tantrums, sulking, or hysterical outbursts. Not surprisingly, such behaviors are not viewed favorably in office situations.

In assessing a person's emotional intelligence five factors are generally considered to get an overall picture:

"No man ever listened himself out of a job." >>> Calvin Coolidge

Your Self-Knowledge: Are you aware of how you are coming across or are you often surprised to hear that you have offended, frightened, or insulted someone else?

Your Ability to Self-Motivate: Are you proactive in deciding what needs to be done or do you sit around like a sullen teenager waiting to be told what is required of you on a regular basis?

Your Ability to Manage Relationships: Are you able to maintain smooth, mature relations with all your coworkers regardless of how you feel about them, or do you become engaged in personal dramas with enemies whom you "hate" or "despise"?

Your Ability to Control Your Moods: Can you keep your moods in check and retain a professional demeanor, or is your inclination to telegraph your foul mood to everyone so no one will mess with you every time you're having a bad day?

Your Ability to Empathize: Are you aware of how others may be feeling and how your actions may affect them, or is your attitude simply that if others don't like what you have to say, that's their problem?

HIGHER
E.I.
ASAP
PLEASE

Hopefully, you can tell from the list above which qualities are indicative of emotional intelligence and which ones are indicative of an emotional moron. And it should come as no surprise that those with a high level of EI tend to lead happier, healthier, and more contented lives, while their less evolved counterparts tend to struggle in all aspects of life as they create their own chaos and immediately set out to cast blame on someone else, the "system," or authority figures in general.

The simple point is that somewhere along the line, between seventh grade and your current situation, the rules changed. Regardless of your qualifications, you will be going nowhere in a big hurry if you behave like an overgrown child. Though this may seem painfully obvious to most of us, an amazing number of people simply never learn to control their emotions, are incapable of communicating clearly, or simply refuse to cooperate. The good side to that is that these people usually end up sabotaging themselves and that makes it easier for the rest of us to move up. But, just for the record, let's sample a few sound bytes that we might hear if we were able to listen in on the internal monologues of two employees on opposite ends of the scale:

LOW EI: Your life is something that happens to you.

HIGH EI: Your life is the result of your choices.

LOW EI: Drama is inevitable and you have to fight back.

HIGH EI: Drama is unnecessary and easily avoided.

LOW EI: I don't know how to do this. I can't let anyone find out.

HIGH EI: I don't know how to do this. Who should I ask?

LOW EI: My boss is an idiot. I am totally screwed.

HIGH EI: My boss is an idiot. This could work to my advantage.

LOW EI: If someone yells at you, you have to yell back.

HIGH EI: If someone yells at you, stare them down and let them fall apart.

LOW EI: If you're overwhelmed, you can't help but freak out.

HIGH EI: If you're overwhelmed, delegate.

LOW EI: The person who questioned my work is an asshole. I hate him.

HIGH EI: The person who questioned my work is mistaken.

LOW EI: Everyone here is out to get me.

HIGH EI: Everyone here can be had.

LOW EI: The boss is drunk. Where're my contra-
ceptives?

HIGH EI: The boss is drunk. Where's my camera?

Slackers and Workaholics

So, you're going to keep yourself in check and you're going to remain calm. You're going to focus on the essentials and you're not going to be swept away in an emotional frenzy. These are good rules to live by. But being honest with ourselves is also required in order to truthfully evaluate our chances for advancement and our responsibility for the situations in which we find ourselves. As always, a life lived on the extremes tends to have repercussions. Are you doing too little, or are you trying to do too much?

TEN SIGNS THAT YOU ARE A SLACKER:

❖ You have more blogs and entertainment websites bookmarked on your computer than work-related sites.

❖ You look forward to deadlines primarily to hear the whooshing sound they make as they fly by.

❖ You are genuinely offended when someone gives you an assignment that is due that same day.

❖ You delete all e-mails on which you are not listed as the primary addressee.

❖ Upon hearing of an April 1st deadline, your assumption is that work on said project should commence on March 31st.

❖ You consider arriving at the office within thirty minutes of the assumed arrival time to be "on time."

❖ You take up smoking specifically to justify more break times.

❖ Your to-do list usually looks very similar on Friday to the way it looked on Monday.

❖ You do not recognize the names of any of the superiors above your own boss.

❖ You consider fire drills a welcome opportunity to mingle with coworkers.

TEN SIGNS THAT YOU ARE A WORKAHOLIC:

❖ You believe that you must respond to every single e-mail that passes through your inbox, even mass e-mails.

❖ Due to a fear of missing crucial information, you regularly try to get in on meetings to which you were not invited.

❖ You will actually run through the workplace rather than be just a few minutes late.

❖ The sight of other employees casually conversing and relaxing fills you with suspicion and hatred.

❖ You feel uneasy and nervous when everything goes smoothly and everyone else is calm and relaxed.

❖ You wake up early to log on and check your e-mails before you get to work.

❖ You log back on at night to make sure you didn't miss anything by leaving too early.

❖ Vacations fill you with anxiety, and your first thought upon arriving at the hotel is "Where can I access the internet?"

❖ You never see friends and your lover is losing interest in you at the speed of light.

❖ You consider fire drills to be an outrageous waste of valuable work time.

Beware the Dreaded Frazzers

Do you sometimes find yourself frazzing? Do you work with a chronic frazzer? The term, coined by psychiatrist and author Edward Hallowell in his book *Crazy Busy: Overstretched, Overbooked and About to Snap—Strategies for Coping in a World Gone ADD*, is defined as: "Frantic, ineffective multitasking, typically with the delusion that you are getting a lot done. The quality of work, however, is poor."

We all know these people. They are constantly plugged in like wide-eyed, techno-age junkies and terrified of losing contact. If they're on a conference call, you can be sure they are also typing away, checking e-mails, and sending instant messages to other people on the call. In meetings they are usually fiddling with some new handheld device until the urge to step outside for some crucial cell phone call overwhelms them. And if you pass by their workspace, their computer screen will be filled with a myriad of open windows, countless e-mails, and God-knows-what-else. Amusingly, such people are actually convinced that their perpetually crazed busyness is a sign of supreme competence and efficiency. They could not be more wrong.

Multiple studies have shown that those who engage in excessive, manic multitasking are far less efficient than those who tackle one task at a time. This is a surprise? Is it not self-evident that those who try to stay on top of everything are ultimately unable to stay on top of anything? Could Michelangelo have ever finished the Sistine Chapel if he was constantly scampering down the

Undo Dread/Despair

scaffolding to hack another piece of marble from an unfinished statue before racing off to sketch a few more nobles? No. The simple fact is that nothing of value has ever been created without some degree of concentration and focus.

Of course, it could be argued that in a frantic society such as the one in which we live no one has the luxury of time to be entirely concentrated on a single task for an unusually extended period of time. But to make oneself so busy that one cannot even retain focus for more than a matter of minutes is to render oneself utterly useless. The truth is that a multitasking addict does little more than create swirl as they frantically try to keep up with what everyone else is doing, when in actuality they rarely achieve or contribute anything of value on their own.

Oh, sure, these whirlwinds of activity may be part of a team that accomplishes something, or they may be involved in some great creation, but deep down inside they know that they have contributed very little, and this only fuels their insecurities and feelings of guilt so that they feel even more compelled to answer those e-mails immediately, pick up the phone on the first ring, or double-book themselves for meetings they are terrified of missing. Such an existence of fear, panic, and neurosis is neither to be admired nor emulated.

In a truly comical attempt to manage employee focus some companies have even gone so far as to encourage their employees to wear different colored hats to signify those times when they may and may not be interrupted. Just picture it. And even more absurdly, it has been reported that there are actually internet software companies working to develop technologies that will help to determine the urgency, prioritize, and even delay incoming e-mails and phone calls based upon organizational flow charts that detail hierarchical relationships between senders and receivers. Can you imagine the cacophony of electronic communications related to that little enterprise?

Now, while these basket cases of which we speak do make for a good chuckle, the unfortunate thing for those who work with them is that they are the ones who end up doing all the work. And though that may seem disheartening, it is important to recognize that there is far greater dignity in being a person who can think, prioritize, and execute by use of the brain than in being a useless typhoon of activity, incapable of living without technological assistance and self-induced crisis.

That said, it is important to point out that a little multitasking is not a bad thing. It can stimulate the mind and actually improve efficiency when practiced in moderation. However, when the

"Politics is the art of looking for trouble, finding it whether it exists or not, diagnosing it incorrectly, and applying the wrong remedy."
>>> Ernest Benn

"frazzing" becomes so all-consuming that you find yourself in a permanent state of anxiety, unable to focus, and panicked at the mere thought of having your electronic communications cut off, you are drifting into dangerous territory. If this applies to you, you can begin to address this sickness by taking a few simple steps.

STEPS TO REGAIN YOUR SANITY:

* Put on the blinders. Commit to one task at a time and finish it before moving on.

* Turn off the sounds on your computer that signify incoming communications. If you feel you are at everyone's beck and call, it's your own fault.

* Turn off your electronic devices when driving or traveling. Try thinking during those times.

* Let your telephone answering service do its job, then review your messages when time allows.

* Don't bring handheld devices to meetings. You'll miss key points and end up sending more e-mails in order to catch up on that which you missed.

* Schedule quiet, uninterrupted time both before and after work.

* Look into getting a life.

Fun Ways to Mess with Your Coworkers

Sometimes the crushing boredom of life at the office requires a little creativity to make things more interesting. You can't just wait around for something to happen, and an inspired employee will always find ways to create a little theatre or social experiment out of an otherwise dull scenario. Here are a few ideas to get you started:

INCREASE YOUR STATURE: Arrive early at the conference room and lower all the adjustable chairs except your own by three inches.

MAKE THEM SQUIRM: After a particularly drunken office holiday party create a fake screen name and identity from another department and send coworkers messages like, "I thought we had a good time. Why haven't you called?"

FREAK SOMEONE OUT: Leave a small gift-wrapped box unattended in the kitchen with a note inside that reads: "We all knew you'd be the one who'd steal this."

MAKE THE BOSS THINK: Send an empty envelope to your boss with an official-looking return address from "The Life Fulfillment Center."

LOOSEN UP A STIFFIE: Log on to the website of a

swinger's resort and sign a coworker up for the free brochure or e-mail updates. (Do this from home on your own computer—remember: Big Brother.)

TORMENT THE EMPLOYEE WHO RELIES ON POST-IT NOTES: Over time, add new ones every now and again with useless phone numbers, dates, and no names.

CREATE AN INTROSPECTIVE QUANDARY: Drop a few quarters in the urinal—enough for a bag of chips.

A SPECIAL PLACE IN HELL . . .

. . . is reserved for that person who approaches as you are eating a bag of chips from the vending machine that only contains five chips to begin with and asks, "Oooh! Can I have one?"

Backstabbers, Networkers, and Users

It's to be expected. There's at least one in every office. There are people in this world who see life as a combative struggle and believe that advancement comes from trickery, deceit, and the crushing of the competition. And while such people can be a royal pain in the ass at work, you must always remember that the same attitude probably exists in their home life, their personal relationships, and every other aspect of their lives. Do not allow yourself to get sucked into their struggles.

When dealing with a toxic coworker, it is best to keep in mind the wisdoms of the masters. Martin Luther King, Jr., the Dalai Lama, and Ghandi all believed in the same principle: If you treat someone like an enemy, they will become your enemy. It's very simple. So, rather than trying to outmaneuver or take revenge on such a character, take a step back and focus on your own mindset.

Of course, it's also important to remember that there is a lot of wiggle room between friend and enemy. No good can come from trying to befriend a miserable, scheming wretch. But sinking down to the level of hating is exhausting and unnecessary. It takes an awful lot of energy to hate someone, and it gives that person great power over you. So, before you hand over the reins ask yourself if the person is really worthy of such an emotional investment on your part. Chances are that they aren't.

That said, it is also your responsibility to protect yourself from being used, taken advantage of, or stabbed in the back. And again, by refusing to be lured into a contest of wills or some twisted

> "A committee is a cul-de-sac down which ideas are lured and then quietly strangled."
> >>> Sir Barnett Cocks

"Never
interrupt
your enemy
when he is
making a
mistake."
>>> Napoleon
Bonaparte

revenge drama, you're half-way there. But beyond that there are a few other things to keep in mind:

▲ You can always meet with your supervisor to discuss any serious issues. (Unless, of course, your supervisor is the problem, in which case a trip upstairs may be in order.)

▲ It's not high school—be professional even if they are not.

▲ Discuss the situation with the coworkers you trust.

▲ Calmly point out any mistruths or misrepresentations if they affect you directly.

▲ Do not get involved in disputes between others, except perhaps to lend an ear to a friend.

▲ Trust in the collective unconscious. More than likely, others are seeing what you are seeing.

▲ Be patient. The best revenge lies in sitting back and watching someone sink their own boat.

Passive-Aggressive Communications

In an era of PC office behavior in which everyone is terrified of making a misstep, many in the workplace attempt to conceal their bullying natures or lazy attitudes by composing delightfully demure e-mails that are, in fact, demands in disguise. While the novice may be lured into such traps, a seasoned office worker knows how to deflect such amateurish attempts at manipulation.

Fending off passive-aggressive e-mails and requests from coworkers may require a little practice, but the effort is well worth it. Once you get comfortable it becomes very easy to nip those sickly-sweet, nonthreatening demands right in the little pink bud. All it takes is a swift turn of the tables that leaves the attacker with no wiggle room.

Consider the following e-mail as an example of a passive-aggressive coworker, whom we shall call "Beatrizia," who is coyly attempting to dump some new work on you. Because the request is not direct, but rather implied, it affords you the perfect out:

THEM:

Hey Michael,

Regarding today's meeting, it would be really great if we could get those reports broken down by state and have the data presented in an easy-to-read spreadsheet or chart for next week's conference.
Thoughts?

Beatrizia

YOU:

> Hi Beatrizia,
>
> I completely agree. Having the info in a simpler format will be so much better.
> Thanks for handling,
>
> Michael

You see? If Beatrizia wants help, Beatrizia shouldn't play games, now should she?

Let's try another one. In this case "Andrew" is angling for some free assistance:

THEM:

> Michael,
>
> I'm hoping you can help me out. My team is in desperate need of someone to write up a simple training tutorial for the new TTR system. I wouldn't normally ask, but you're such a good writer, and I'm hoping this wouldn't be too big an imposition?
> Lemme know,
>
> Andrew

YOU:

Hey Andrew,

I'd love to help you out, but unfortunately, I haven't been trained in TTR yet. I'm scheduled for a class next month if you can wait that long. If not, I happen to know that Beatrizia has had the training.

Michael

See? A nice slice return of the ping-pong ball and you can take them both out. It's really just a matter of understanding human nature. The way people behave in the workplace is usually a reflection of how they operate in the world at large. Annoying impositions or awkward attempts to seek help are not necessarily signs of malice or selfishness, but it's always best to protect oneself by assessing the message behind the message. Dissecting the psychology of your coworkers can be good fun in and of itself, but it is also a worthy endeavor to ensure that others are not taking advantage of you.

5

Corporate Lingo

"Do not accustom yourself
to use big words
for little matters."
>>> Samuel Johnson

Say What?

IN ANY TYPE OF CORPORATION OR LARGE company a strange phenomenon exists that has only grown more prevalent in recent years. Though the specifics and the terminology may vary depending upon the nature of the business, the effect remains the same. We are referring here to the rise of corporate double-speak, which can loosely be defined as empty, meaningless communications intended to create an impression of progress and productivity. In fact, such communications are usually employed to conceal a lack of both.

The workplace equivalent of The Emperor's New Clothes, corporate double-speak may manifest itself in the spoken word or it may involve typing, but regardless of the form it requires keen interpretation.

Have you ever received an e-mail along these lines?

Hi all,

Attached please find the creative solutions delivered by the agency that Outsource Management hired. The solutions were created with PPB approvals in mind for crediting both XM and cobranded partners with RLs and the Systems Task Force for the requirements that I have previously outlined, however they have not gone through JMD review yet. They are going to review the proposed designs solutions with the Conceptual Integration Manager first (he could not make the meeting today) then submit to XM/PPB/STF for approval. Not all executions are presented (as input from Lars and the SSP team has been delayed due to the new baby—Ha Ha—Congratulations!), but rest assured they will apply same rules once PQS has fully vetted the proposal. If MMX does not circle back with a sign-off, they will tweak. Marketing is submitting and managing approvals directly with Mindy and we anticipate increasing traction on the TG as the RS team continues to perform with AWESOME efficiency.

Questions? Lemme know.

Idiot

(**Translation:** Lars' wife had a baby and the project is fucked.)

Sadly, this faux e-mail will ring a bell with anyone who ever worked within a large corporation. Of course any sane person will recognize that the

Delete
BS

abuse of acronyms and internal language is a mere disguise for slow progress and general panic. Still, many of us are subjected daily to curious e-mail puzzles that could not be interpreted by even the most advanced cyber-chiatrists. Such is the tragedy of techno-speak and corporate jargon.

An e-mail of this nature is impossible to respond to or act upon, and so the wise employee will simply sit back with a bag of popcorn and watch the show.

Corporate Buzzwords and the Fools Who Use Them

You know who they are. Those entirely incompe-tent, disorganized or psychotic, coworkers who need to disguise their inefficiency with the ridicu-lous jargon also known as MBA-speak. Now, you and I know that there are certain phrases that inspire cringes and askew glances in the con-ference room when tossed about with unseemly abandon. To be fair we all inadvertently cough up a doozy from time to time, but it is those who spew them forth regularly that truly deserve our collective contempt because they are all euphemisms intended to conceal heart-stopping insecurity and a staggering lack of self-awareness. The people who embrace a hideously clichéd vocabulary of corporate buzzwords are rarely aware of the snickers and contempt they incite.

If you want to get ahead in the corporate world, you will be doing yourself a great favor if you avoid these transparent attempts to seem "professional." That shit fools no one, though it is quite amusing to overhear the person in the next pod solemnly intoning: "I'll circle back with you on that after I speak with my colleague who has been very proactive regarding deliverables related to that initiative." Translation: "I have no idea what you're talking about."

Presumably, if you have been hired by a large corporation, you have received a reasonable education and you should have a decent vocabulary to go with it. Use it. Your superiors will be amazed at your magical "personal touch," and your ability to "connect" with people. Say what you mean—employing diplomacy of course—and at all costs resist the following phrases that will only mark you as a pretentious suck-up:

ACTION ITEM (noun): An actual task to be placed on a list of actual tasks to be done.

Example of usage: "I'll come up with a list of action items after the meeting."

True meaning: "I'm not doing it, but I'll send you an e-mail of things that need to be done."

BADLY SOURCED (adjective): Having been informed by inaccurate or questionable data.

Example of usage: "Unfortunately, that report was badly sourced."

True meaning: "The report was wrong."

BASIC AGREEMENT (noun): A preliminary understanding between interested parties.

Example of usage: "I've reached a basic agreement with the sales department on that."

True meaning: "The bastards haven't answered my e-mail yet."

BEST PRACTICES (noun): Efficient processes shared amongst coworkers.

Example of usage: "Perhaps someone could circulate a list of best practices?"

True meaning: "I don't know how the hell to do this. How do you do it?"

CAPTURE "ASKS" (verb): To compile a list of requests.

Example of usage: "We have captured some of the asks from our last meeting."

True meaning: "This time, I wrote the shit down."

CHALLENGE (noun) : An obstacle or problem yet to be addressed.

> *Example of usage:* "There are still some challenges with this project we're looking into."
>
> *True meaning:* "It's not do-able. I'm going to dump this in someone else's lap."

CIRCLE BACK (verb) : To revisit or follow up at a future point in time.

> *Example of usage:* "Let me look into that and I'll circle back with you in a week or two."
>
> *True meaning:* "I'm going to drop this stink-bomb and hope you forget about it."

CLIENT CREATIVE (noun) : A concrete example of a proposed design or advertisement.

> *Example of usage:* "We're awaiting sign-off on the client creative."
>
> *True meaning:* "The ad sucks."

CORE COMPETENCY (noun) : A primary strength or an area in which the greatest success is usually found.

> *Example of usage:* "The core competency of our group lies in our ability to identify areas for potential improvement and leverage our assets to implement solutions."
>
> *True meaning:* "We are best at guessing and stealing ideas."

Decode
Odious
E-Mail

CORPORATE VISION (noun) : A distributed definition of a company's collective self-image and mission.

> *Example of usage:* "Your proposal really doesn't adhere to the corporate vision."
>
> *True meaning:* "Your ideas are creative and new. We hate that."

DELIVERABLE (noun) : An element or feature of a product that is forthcoming.

> *Example of usage:* "We are working on those deliverables right now."
>
> *True meaning:* "We haven't started on the things we promised you last month."

DISCONNECT (noun) : A misunderstanding or error in communication between groups or individuals.

> *Example of usage:* "There must have been some disconnect between marketing and sales."
>
> *True meaning:* "We really should think about introducing the sales and marketing staffs."

DIVERSITY AWARENESS/TRAINING (noun) : Sensitivity training offered to combat workplace discrimination and/or sexual harassment.

> *Example of usage:* "Bill has shown great interest in the diversity training courses."
>
> *True meaning:* "Bill is a racist."

DRILL DOWN (verb): To increase detail or further examine at a deeper level.

> *Example of usage:* "We'll need to drill down a bit further to fully analyze this data."
>
> *True meaning:* "I have no idea what these numbers mean."

HUH?

EMPOWER (verb): To improve morale of subordinates by delegating responsibility and opportunity.

> *Example of usage:* "By handing this project off to you, I'm hoping to empower you a bit more."
>
> *True meaning:* "I'm dumping my work on you, but you can't complain because I used the word 'empower,' so if you complain, that's a 'bad attitude.'"

EXCITING TIMES (adjective with noun): A time of great promise, enthusiasm, and hope.

> *Example of usage:* "We are entering exciting times, and I foresee great things for all of us."
>
> *True meaning:* "This boat is sinking."

FACE TIME (noun): Personal interaction and open communications between coworkers or supervisors and subordinates.

> *Example of usage:* "I'm hoping to have more face time with you going forward."
>
> *True meaning:* "If you're late one more time, I'm canning your ass."

FAST TRACK (noun or verb): An accelerated move of an employee up the corporate ladder.

Example of usage: "That little receptionist is certainly on a fast track."

True meaning: "That little receptionist is definitely blowing somebody."

FIRE DRILL (noun): An emergency or urgent situation requiring immediate attention.

Example of usage: "Sorry about the fire drill, everyone, but we really need to get this out the door."

True meaning: "I totally forgot about this, and now I need you all to drop your work and save my ass."

FLAGPOLE (noun): A symbolic device by which prevailing winds of thought may be measured.

Example of usage: "That's a great idea, Sam. Let's run it up the flagpole in tomorrow's meeting."

True meaning: "That's a stupid idea, Sam, but I'm not going to be the one to shoot it down. Let's make it a public spectacle."

LEVERAGE (verb): A pretentious word meaning to "use."

Example of usage: "We can leverage your expertise on this subject along with her writing skills."

True meaning: "I will be stealing ideas from both of you."

LOW-HANGING FRUIT (noun): That which is desirable and easily accessible.

Example of usage: "There's a lot of low-hanging fruit here that we are hoping to take advantage of."

True meaning: "Let's focus on the easy stuff that requires no effort."

METRIC (noun): Any unit of measurement.

Example of usage: "I'd love to see some metrics from you that reflect your progress."

True meaning: "I don't really believe you do anything here. Prove it."

OFF-LINE (adjective): An arena or milieu other than the one in which you find yourself.

Example of usage: "That's an interesting observation, Louis. Let's discuss that off-line."

True meaning: "Don't ever embarrass me like that in public again!"

OUT OF THE LOOP (adjective): A state of non-inclusion.

Example of usage: "I'm afraid I must have been out of the loop on that conversation."

True meaning: "No one told me! It's not my fault!"

OPEN-DOOR POLICY (noun): An availability and interest in the problems, ideas, or opinions of subordinates.

Example of usage: "I encourage you all to take advantage of my open-door policy."

True meaning: "If the building's on fire, come and let me know. Otherwise, fuck off."

OUTSIDE THE BOX (adjective): Beyond the ordinary and predictable, especially in relation to creative ideas.

Example of usage: "I love your way of thinking outside the box. It's very refreshing."

True meaning: "You are a nut job and you're getting on my nerves."

OUTSOURCING (noun): The practice of transferring work to outside companies or organizations.

Example of usage: "We're looking at some exciting opportunities for outsourcing that will make all our jobs much easier."

True meaning: "I strongly recommend that you update your resumes."

PLATE (noun): A metaphor for the size of one's workload.

Example of usage: "I'd do it myself, but I have a lot on my plate at the moment."

True meaning: "You do it."

POTENTIAL SHOW STOPPER (noun): A problem or "challenge" that might potentially derail a project.

Example of usage: "Well, if the designs aren't delivered on time, that could be a potential show stopper."
True meaning: "If this thing goes belly up, it's the art department's fault!"

RESOURCES (noun): As in human resources, the amount of people-power associated with a project.

Example of usage: "It sounds like an exciting idea if we can get the appropriate resources allocated to the project."
True meaning: "Okay, but I'm not doing this myself. I'll need other people to actually do the work."

RESTRUCTURING (noun or verb): An internal reorganization of staff usually including layoffs and increased workloads for those lucky enough to remain in the fold.

Example of usage: "After thoroughly reviewing the situation we feel that a complete restructuring will streamline efficiencies and create a more seamless workflow for all involved."
True meaning: "They're onto us, so we have to shuffle the deck and throw a few sandbags off of this balloon ride."

SIGN-OFF (noun or verb): An official "okay" from a superior or coworker required for a project to proceed.

> "He can compress the most words into the smallest idea of any man I know."
> >>> Abraham Lincoln

DID YOU KNOW?

The term "red tape" was first used to describe bureaucracy by Charles Dickens. He was referring to the red cloth tape that British lawyers and government officials used to bind documents together.

Example of usage: "We just wanted to get your sign-off on these plans before we move to the next step."

True meaning: "We just want to ensure that you'll have to take the blame if the shit hits the fan."

SKEWING TOWARD (verb): A shift in trends, usually in reference to some form of measurement.

Example of usage: "In reviewing the numbers we found that the overall trend is skewing toward a younger, hipper audience."

True meaning: "You geeks have been barking up the wrong tree."

TASK FORCE (noun): An assembly of unrelated employees designated to perform some vague task that no one wants to deal with.

Example of usage: "You've been chosen to head the mailroom efficiencies task force!"

True meaning: "I know you're not doing anything and I'm going to punish you for it."

TOUCH BASE (verb): An act of minimal contact wherein acknowledgement is given that a certain subject will eventually have to be dealt with.

Example of usage: "Absolutely! Let's touch base on that later."

True meaning: "Can you not see that I'm busy?"

WIN/WIN (adjective): A term to describe a situation in which there is no loser.

>   *Example of usage:* "It's a win/win situation!"
>   *True meaning:* "You lose."

Corporate Buzzword Bingo

Given the wealth of idiotic terminology that gets lobbed about in the average corporate meeting, an amusing little diversion has recently become popular. It is known as Corporate Buzzword Bingo, and it can be played by two or more attendees at any given meeting. It may be played for fun, for money, or for any other prize upon which the participants agree. The rules are simple, but stealth is often required to conceal the playing of the game.

In advance of the meeting, each player draws a grid of sixteen squares on a page and a list of sixteen terms is distributed. Each player places the distributed terms in the squares in an arrangement of their own choosing. During the course of the meeting, an "X" is placed on each term as it is coughed up by the unwitting speakers. The first to complete a row of four squares (either horizontally, vertically, or diagonally) wins.

Of course, it is not a particularly good idea to scream "BINGO!" during a meeting, so the players need to agree upon some cue to indicate victory. Recommended: A big fake sneeze:

ACHOO!!! = *I won, suckahs!*

SAMPLE:

CIRCLE BACK	SYNERGY	LEVERAGE	OFF-LINE
SIGN-OFF	METRICS	OUT OF/ IN THE LOOP	DISCONNECT
TOUCH BASE	DELIVERABLE	RESTRUCTURE	FIRE DRILL
FAST TRACK	ACTION ITEM	EMPOWER	CHALLENGE

New Terms for Common Office Phenomena

While great fun can be had mocking the absurd linguistic gymnastics of one's coworkers, there is also a new vocabulary emerging that is far more likely to be employed by those situated more closely to the bottom of the power pyramid than the top.

Chances are that each of these little gems will trigger some degree of recognition:

ADMINISPHERE: The vague and hard-to-pinpoint upper organizational layers from which bad ideas, unexpected directives, and mysterious new rules fall like unwelcome confetti upon the heads of those below.

ASSMOSIS: The process by which shameless employees seek to absorb information and advance themselves by disgracefully kissing up to the boss.

BANALYSIS: The use of excessive charts, documentation, or implied theory to state the painfully obvious.

BLAMESTORMING: A collective bitchfest during which office failures or missed deadlines are analyzed and scapegoats are identified.

BLANDIOSE: The manner in which grand statements or attempts at inspiration are delivered in sleep-inducing tones by a charisma-free speaker.

CORPORANUS: An employee who insists on adhering strictly to procedure and is unreasonably committed to the company.

CROPDUSTING: The unseemly habit of farting as one quickly passes through the collective workspace, leaving coworkers glaring at one another suspiciously.

CUBE FARM: An office space consisting primarily of cubicles.

DRINK THE KOOL-AID: The act of buying into a corporate philosophy and becoming a mindless cheerleader for that message.

EDUBABBLE: A pretentious form of speech peppered with esoteric references and lofty allusions used to describe simple concepts. Intended to impress, it usually results in stifled giggles.

EGO WALL: The wall on which an employee hangs their various degrees, awards, and photos of themselves in which they have successfully ambushed celebrities.

ETERNITY LEAVE: Time off granted to an employee who is ushering a loved one to the other side.

GRANNY LEAVE: Time taken off under the pretense of having an ailing grandmother.

LAYOFF LUST: An overwhelming, deeply passionate desire to be laid off.

MOUSE POTATO: The online equivalent of yesterday's couch potato.

MUCUS TROOPER: An employee who heroically and annoyingly shows up for work despite a raging cold or flu.

OPEN THE KIMONO: To reluctantly reveal the accounting books in the face of an investigation.

PERCUSSIVE MAINTENANCE: An attempt to fix a technical problem by banging on or flat-out assaulting an electronic device of any kind.

PRAIRIE DOGGING: The effect seen in a cube farm when a loud noise or a major system malfunction causes employees to pop up and look around in the manner of prairie dogs.

PREVENGE: An act of revenge taken in anticipation of an impending confrontation or slight.

RECTAL DATABASE: The mysterious location from which sudden solutions, related data, or anecdotes from the past are miraculously retrieved. The conference-room equivalent of magically pulling a rabbit out of one's ass.

SALMON DAY: A day spent struggling valiantly against the current, in hopes of succeeding only to get screwed and die in the end.

SEAGULL MANAGER: A manager who swoops into an existing situation, makes a great deal of noise, shits on everything, and then disappears.

SILVER CEILING: An invisible barrier in the modern workplace preventing the promotion and professional advancement of gray-haired employees.

TECHNOSEXUAL: A seemingly asexual employee who becomes unreasonably excited or worked up only in the face of a technological breakthrough or the discovery of a new functionality.

UNINSTALLED: The state of having been fired.

Assuming that you yourself have yet to be uninstalled, there are still more lessons to learn and corporate concepts to consider. Let us proceed.

CHAPTER

6

Death by PowerPoint

"There is a time for
many words, and there is
also a time for sleep."
>>> Homer

The Corporate Sleeping Pill

MEETINGS ARE AN INTEGRAL PART OF ANY successful business model. They are a means by which employees gather to exchange ideas, agree upon directions, plot strategies, reach agreements, give voice to concerns, air grievances, and share successes and news. At their best they can be entirely engaging, encourage participation, result in inspiration, and even be entertaining. Unfortunately, such meetings are usually the exception to the rule, and the further up the ladder you climb, the more useless meetings you get dragged into.

You know the ones. You're buried in work and trying desperately to catch up, but you are repeatedly required to attend meetings and conference calls during which the speaker is usually the least charismatic person available and the struggle to fend off a complete collapse of consciousness becomes all-consuming. Ironically, the meetings themselves are often called to address lists of projects that are behind schedule because everyone is too busy going to meetings to actually get any work done. And yet, we grab our pens and notebooks and trudge along, dead-faced, to the conference room.

In fact, it is actually possible to have a high-paying career that consists entirely of attending meetings. If the boss gets invited to enough of them, he or she can create the illusion of being involved in everything without actually having to accomplish anything. Well, anything other than calling a meeting with the staff to outline what needs to be done.

Oftentimes, PowerPoint slide shows reiterating the agenda items you already saw in the invitation e-mail are addressed one by one in excruciating detail. In the worst cases the dullard at the helm merely reads from the slide, and then proceeds to state the obvious. By the time he or she has finished elaborating on the first point the whole team has read all the bullet points on the slide and silent, psychic screams of "WE GET IT!" are flying about the room.

Not surprisingly, the longer the presentation, the more the energy is sucked right out of the audience and by the time the speaker asks if there are any questions there is usually an extended and highly uncomfortable silence as few have the energy left to ask a question, let alone keep their foreheads from crashing to the table. It's all very . . . stupid. However, there are things that each of us can do to lessen the tedium regardless of whether we are giving the presentation or suffering through it.

DID YOU KNOW?

ZZZZZZZZZ
According to a study by MCI, Inc:

91 percent of employees admit to daydreaming during meetings.

73 percent admit bringing other work to meetings.

39 percent admit to having fallen asleep in meetings.

For the Presenter

If you have been tapped to lead a meeting you will be doing everyone involved a great favor if you make an attempt to mix things up just a bit. There are things that will work to your advantage, and things to be avoided at all costs:

PRESENTATION DOs:

Do Keep It Brief: Do not fall prey to the idea that longer is better, or that you are impressing anyone with a series of lengthy soliloquies. A clean, clear, and structured meeting will only make you appear supremely organized and refreshingly focused. Make an agenda and stick to it.

Do Invite Others to Contribute: Give them advanced notice that you will call on them, but have coworkers address whatever is in their area of expertise. It will keep people alert for their moment in the sun and at the very least will mix up the voices and allow people to turn their heads occasionally.

Do Use Humor: This does not mean relying on corny jokes, but by simply being honest and light-hearted about potential pitfalls or past blunders you will put others at ease. If you are not naturally funny, try including whimsical images of monkeys or dogs doing silly things in your slides.

Do Try to Relax: You are not being presented to the Queen. By loosening up and trying to enjoy yourself you'll be less paranoid about tiny mistakes and less likely to trip yourself up. People always relate better to watching a human being rather than an employee-on-a-stick.

Do Focus on the Positive: Corny though it may seem, you will keep the audience on your side if you avoid any mentions whatsoever that may sound accusatory or those that imply blame. No one needs rifts or enemies, and if you've been asked to do the presentation, chances are you have a stake in the proceedings and you'll be the one who ultimately benefits the most from smooth sailing.

Do Make an Effort to Look Decent: This doesn't mean dressing like it's your first day of Sunday school, but if you make an effort, you'll feel a bit more comfortable and confident up there. Besides, audiences are rarely inspired by someone who looks as if they just crawled out of a dumpster.

PRESENTATION DON'Ts:

Don't Open with Precious Anecdotes: Really. Please save the adorable stories about the things you learned from your three-year-old for the in-laws. It's all very precious, but that's not really what all these people are here for, is it? The same applies to the lessons you learned on your first paper route or the perky slogans you learned from your sorority sisters.

Don't Play Schoolmarm: Do not call on people like schoolchildren asking them to define terms or provide examples. Open questions are fine, but pop quizzes rarely go over well with coworkers.

Don't Keep Repeating Yourself: Be aware of constantly repeating tedious questions with every new topic such as, "What do we mean by this?" or "Why is this important?" By doing so you are contributing to the general drowsiness in the room and cannot, therefore, feel sorry for yourself when there are no questions.

Don't Bury Them in Corporate Speak: Do not attempt to impress by using company buzzwords, techno-speak or confusing your audience by using endless acronyms that they don't even understand. By doing so you are merely setting yourself up for a very lonely time at the holiday party.

Don't Expect High-Fives and Cheers: Natural enthusiasm happens spontaneously and is usually appreciated, but if you drift over the line and find yourself pacing the room like a football coach or encouraging others to "get psyched," . . . well, it's just going to be very embarrassing for everyone. Don't do that.

For the Attendees

As was previously stated, not all meetings are deathly boring. If you're lucky, your interest will be piqued, new ideas will come your way, and you may leave with a better understanding of what you need to do. If not, there's always Buzzword Bingo. And there are also a few dos and don'ts that may help keep you engaged and might even score you a few points:

MEETING DOs:

Do Arrive on Time: It will mark you as reliable, but far more importantly it will allow you to avoid getting the seat right up front or by that awful person next to whom no one else wishes to sit.

Do Take Notes: Jot down a few things that you might refer to later for questions. You never know when you might be called upon, and if you like the speaker at all, you can do him or her a favor by asking a question when the silence gets unbearable.

Do Keep Your Eyes on the Presentation: A glazed but focused stare is always preferable in the eyes of the presenter than a downcast head laboring over a doodle. You don't want to scare the speaker with crazy-eyes, but try to feign reasonable interest at the very least. Your boss is probably watching you too.

Do Study the Others in Attendance: Much can be gleaned by observing your coworkers when their defenses are down and a coma is beginning to set in. You'll get a much better read on who takes their job seriously and who is completely checked out.

Do Feel Free to Let Your Mind Wander: As long as you can convincingly appear to be listening, you are entirely free to make the most of the dead time to reflect on other job offers, your next vacation, your grocery list, or what that new employee across the room might look like naked.

MEETING DON'Ts:

Don't Let Your Body Language Betray You: Excessive slumping, heavy eyelids, and backward sprawls make it a little too obvious that you think this whole thing is just a big bag of gas. Try to conceal those thoughts to a reasonable degree.

Don't Suck Up: Contributing to the dialogue and offering up ideas is one thing, but transparent attempts to impress the boss or glean praise for your clever answers will only contribute to a rapid plunge in popularity. Speak up if you have something to say, but don't speak up if you're just angling for a gold star.

Don't Bring Your Cell Phone: It's like the movies. If it goes off it interrupts everything, all heads turn to you, you make a surprised "apology face," your boss will be irritated, and, if you step outside to take it, disapproving glances will soon be darting all over the place.

Don't Engage in Whispered Side Conversations: If the speaker's fly is down, well, of course you'll want to share the glee, but that can be done in a word or two. Ongoing whispery chats are simply rude to the person who's speaking and you'll eventually be drawing awkward, unwanted attention to yourself.

Don't Dart from the Room the Second It's Over: A little social milling about never hurts. Just as you don't want to rush in late, you don't want to sprint out the door when the speaker concludes as if you can no longer breathe. Besides, you'll miss all the snarky comments of your coworkers on the long walk back.

The single most important thing to remember about an office presentation is that everyone's participation is being monitored. If you are an attendee, you cannot afford to be obviously

"Meetings are an addictive, highly self-indulgent activity that corporations and other large organizations habitually engage in only because they cannot actually masturbate."
>>> Dave Barry

"Make sure you have finished speaking before your audience has finished listening."
>>> Dorothy Sarnoff

disinterested. Make an effort and let someone else play the fool by falling asleep. If you are presenting, don't give in to the temptation to fill the silences with endless blather. Seize the stage, have fun, and try to be succinct and clear. Your superiors will marvel at your ability to "engage the team."

Fun Ways to Liven Up a Dull Meeting

Having reviewed the general rules for conference room decorum, it must be acknowledged that sometimes things simply slide into a state of utter absurdity and the urge to stand up and scream becomes overwhelming. But standing up and screaming is not very inspired, nor will it endear you to your colleagues. When the urge to rock the boat becomes irresistible, you might as well have a little fun with it:

❖ Upon arrival, arrange in front of yourself a mug of coffee, a can of Red Bull, a bottle of caffeine pills and eye drops. Then sit up straight and look really interested.

❖ In the middle of the presentation, turn to the person next to you and loudly demand that they stop touching you.

❖ If the speaker refers to a need to increase productivity, yell "You got it!" and sprint from the room.

❖ Raise your hand, and when you're called upon, ask the speaker: "Do you like my hair this way?"

❖ Every time an important point is made, make a small sexual noise like you're building toward an orgasm.

❖ Arrange for someone to call the conference room phone in the middle of the presentation. Pick up the phone, listen for a moment, and say: "Well, I would love to. Shall we say six o'clock? Terrific, I'll see you there. Buh-bye." Hang up and shrug to apologize for the interruption.

❖ Stand by the door as everyone is leaving and thank them for coming.

Internal Activities to Help Pass the Time

If there's no one in the meeting to play with, and you don't want to create a scene, then you'll just have to entertain yourself. When all else fails, games of the mind can be quite entertaining. Just remember to keep an ear open in case your name is called.

❖ Stare at the textured ceiling panels until you see pictures form.

❖ One by one, imagine how each person at the meeting would look after a sex-change operation.

❖ Try to remember every concert you've ever attended.

❖ Do a little math and figure out how many work hours are left until you can retire.

❖ Straighten your legs out under the table and see how long you can keep them extended without touching the ground.

❖ Pit the other attendees against one another in imaginary competitions. Who has the best hair, the best hands, the best teeth, or the best nose?

❖ See if you can make yourself cry.

Conference Calls

As a modern variation on the old-fashioned meeting, conference calls have an etiquette all their own. In most cases more people are invited than are necessary, and this usually affords the caller greater freedom to drift in and out of the proceedings. With your headset firmly in place, there is ample opportunity to tend to other business without seeming rude or disinterested.

YOUR 3-WAY IS WAITING...

While a conference call involving a mere handful of people requires a higher degree of alertness, the inevitable "all-hands" call need not be any more distracting than the music in the elevator. But regardless of the scale there are a few simple rules and tips to remember for any conference call:

▲ Call in a few minutes early. Better to be there early and eavesdrop on the opening chit-chat than arriving late and interrupting the call.

▲ Always mute yourself when not speaking. It will help conceal your distracted typing, unintentional sighs, and moans of disapproval.

▲ Always keep an ear open in case your name is called while you are reading the news or conversing with a friend while muted.

▲ Always have a few notes or numbers ready in case you are called upon to represent your team's progress or your personal insights.

▲ If you are suddenly called upon and have no idea what's being discussed, always blame it on the phone system. "I'm sorry, you were breaking up. Can you repeat the question?"

▲ Open Instant Message windows with friends

who are also on the call. That way you can make snide comments and have an amusing running commentary on the proceedings.

▲ Make an effort to chime in at least once on the call with a question or comment. It will make it seem as if you are actually interested and paying attention, and will lessen the chances of your being ambushed by an unexpected question.

▲ Always let your voice be heard upon sign-off. It will prove that you were there and you listened, regardless of whether that is true or not.

Additionally, it should be pointed out that the phone headset is an ideal way to mislead others and conceal your own lack of productivity. People don't bother people who are on a call, and people don't question a complete lack of activity when someone is on a call. So, if you're too hungover to even type or you're just too checked out to even feign working, simply pop on the headset and look serious. No one will ever question you because no one can ever keep track of all the stupid calls that take place every day. If you can play it off well and blurt out an occasional question, it can buy you up to ninety minutes of alone time.

The Bottom Line

Meetings, no matter how dull or pointless they may be, provide endless opportunities to exercise the mind and score points with your superiors. By seizing control of your own entertainment you can transcend the tedious. By speaking up during the question and answer period you can ingratiate yourself immeasurably in the eyes of the presenter and your boss as well. Always remember that one dumb question will elevate you above all your slacking coworkers in the eyes of those who determine your annual raise. It's well worth the performance.

CHAPTER

7

E-Mail Etiquette and Disasters

"People who work
sitting down get
paid more than people
who work standing up."
>>> Ogden Nash

Pointless Communications

ONE OF THE UNFORTUNATE BY-PRODUCTS OF the great technological advances of recent years is the prevalence in all workplaces of useless e-mails. The immediacy of e-mail communication has ushered in an age of vagaries, impulsive communications, and acronym abuse. Nowadays, workers type up their every thought and fire off e-mails with tremendous inaccuracy or complete pointlessness.

The advent of the ability to carbon copy, or CC, e-mails has only worsened the problem. We are copied on e-mails that do not directly affect us in the vague interest of keeping everyone "in the loop." Do I need to be in the loop? Who else is in the loop? Is there even a need for a loop here? Did you ever notice that the more you type the word "loop," the less you remember what it means? Loop. Loop. Loop. Loooooop. I digress.

The truth is that cyber-communications have taken on a life of their own with ever-evolving techno-speak and the ability to multimessage; communications are devolving rather than improving. Have you checked your own penmanship lately? It's not quite what it used to be, is it? And when was the last time you actually sent someone a hand-written letter? You can't remember, can you? Do you even own a pencil anymore?

The hand-written word has all but been replaced with the typed word. Typing is no longer a skill to be mastered primarily by secretaries and journalists, it has become an essential part of any profession. The mere thought of writing any form of communication without the ability to delete a line, cut-and-paste, or run a spell-check is practically inconceivable to many. And as a result language in general has been transformed at warp speed to incorporate a variety of symbols, acronyms, and silly symbols.

In any given company different departments develop different lingo, and mysterious acronyms are assumed to be universally understood. For any new employee joining a company, a steep learning curve awaits that involves deciphering the various languages that everyone else takes for granted. As technology races ahead, the average worker can only dream of keeping up.

Oddly, much of the currently common workplace vernacular is based on codes and cryptic acronyms developed by teens who embraced the new internet medium much more quickly than their elders. As is the case with learning foreign

DID YOU KNOW?

E-mail was in use as early as 1965, nearly twenty years before the internet came into being.

languages, the young and unformed mind is far more receptive to new languages than a stubborn old brain. And as a result, highly paid corporate executives now engage in teen-speak without batting an eye.

The Assault of the Instant Message

To the modern office employee it is simply unfathomable to think of the days when letters were dictated to secretaries who then typed them up before dropping them in the mail. In the best case scenario your communication would be received two or three days later, and only in the most urgent situations would it be returned immediately. But if you think about it, that is precisely the type of atmosphere in which the standard three-martini lunch became a possibility in the first place.

Sadly, no one has time for even a single martini these days. Communications fly back and forth with such lightning speed that a delay in response of even an hour or two may result in red-faced irritation and clenched fists. And for those who find e-mail to be intolerably slow, instant messaging has become the favored form of passive-aggressive workplace assault. If your coworker is not convinced you will read his or her e-mail immediately, he can simply "ping" you with some adorable little acronym or opener. You know, something like this:

Hi. yt?: This seemingly innocuous little inquiry regarding your whereabouts is in fact a loaded bomb. It usually means: "Oy, drop what you're doing. I need something now!" The inquiry as to whether or not you are there is code for "Are you available?"

qq: This is rarely ever really a "quick question" and it usually involves a shrewdly insinuated request that will not be quickly resolved.

Got a sec?: Of course, everyone has a second to spare, but this innocent little inquiry usually involves many minutes or far worse devoted to some tedious issue and is often followed by a "Can u come over?"

Hey: The vaguest of salutations, this little opener can mean good gossip or an infuriating request. It's pretty much the electronic equivalent of a "box of choc-o-lates."

U alone?: The most promising of all, this greeting implies secrecy and discretion is in order. In most cases that means scandalous gossip, inside information, dirty pictures, or the slagging off of a fellow employee. It's the most day-brightening of all greetings.

OMG: The call to the gods may indicate incoming hilarity or something truly odious. An opener such as this should be met with caution and low expectations.

So . . . : Rarely received from superiors, this one usually comes from friends and is most often indicative of a disgruntled rant or ongoing complaint. It may either be fun or tedious, but it's always a thrilling gamble.

'sup: This can never come from someone worth talking to. People whose workplace vernacular is inspired by beer commercials are rarely important enough to worry about. Close the window.

By clearly assessing the opening salvo of any instant message, you should be able to manage your distractions effectively. Always remember that if they have to ask if "you're there," they probably can't see you. Therefore, you can keep them on hold indefinitely, suggesting the flimsy premise that you are away from your desk tending to something terribly important. It always tips the scales in your direction if you do not answer too quickly. You want to create the impression that, yes they are interrupting—unless, of course, you receive the promising allure of a "u alone?" However, the essential gaining of the upper hand can be achieved in a variety of ways beyond mere stalling. Consider the following easy-peasy options:

otp: By claiming to be "on the phone," you are sending a message that this had better be good. You are also buying time as there is the inherent implication that you may be called upon to speak on the call, thus adding extra awkwardness to the interruption.

Hang on: An all-purpose stalling technique that suggests you are wildly busy in some vague capacity, but you are heroically trying to accommodate the interruptrix.

One sec: It is essential for the "One sec" to be followed by an excruciatingly long pause if it is to be of any use whatsoever. Let the second become a minute at the very least to establish how very busy you are.

I am away and unable to read your message: Only those with lightning reflexes will be able to trigger the "away message" quickly enough for it to be truly plausible. If you can manage to strike the key within a three second window, you might just get away with it.

In the event that you have responded to a seemingly innocuous instant message with a line or two and it suddenly turns out to be an annoying request, do not panic. It is important that you remain in control of the situation and refuse to be yanked around. If you are suddenly ambushed by an urgent question or sent a link that you are expected to examine immediately, simply

DID YOU KNOW?

Approximately thirty-one billion e-mails are sent every day.

Roughly 40 percent of all e-mails are spam.

The average corporate employee sends thirty-four e-mails per day.

The average person has 3.1 e-mail addresses.

lean forward from your reclined position after a sufficient pause and type, "Totally swamped rihgt now, can u sedn in an e-mail?" (the misspellings add a touch of authenticity), then lean back and resume your relaxation.

Though the e-mail will most likely arrive immediately, you will have retained the upper hand and may eventually address the looming issue as time permits.

The Neurotic Closer

Nothing soothes the spirit more than screwing with a neurotic coworker. Therefore, it should be noted that there is a great opportunity for fun and highly satisfying torture in instant messaging or e-mails, especially if you find yourself engaged in communication with a "neurotic closer." This is the person who simply must have the last word in any exchange. It's a rare bird, to be sure, but an opportunity that should not be squandered. The beauty herein lies in the fact that this person simply cannot end an exchange unless they are able to close things out. The possibilities for torment are endless. And it might go something like this:

You: "I'll send that document ASAP."

Them: "Awesome."

You: "No problem."

Them: "Thanks."

You: "You bet."

Them: "Cool."

You: "Comin' your way."

Them: "Gotcha."

You: "Two minutes."

Them: "You rock!"

You: "I do!"

Them: "You're so funny."

You: "Well . . . yeah."

Them: "Ok. Thanks again."

You: "I'll include the spreadsheet."

Them: "Love it."

You: "I aims to please."

Them: "You're a nut."

You: "You think?"

Them: "Totally."

You: "Ok, later."

Them: "Right."

You: "Cya"

Them: "Yep."

You: "Ciao."

Them: "Later."

You: "qq?"

Them: "Yes?"

You: "Never mind."

Them: "No, what?"

You: "It's nothing."

Them: "What?"

You: "Forget it. Spreadsheet comin' your way."

Them: "Coolio."

You: "YGM."

Them: "Thx."

You: "Byeeeeeeeeeeee!"

By this point your intended victim will be in a swollen-headed, sweaty tizzy and you can abruptly head off for an extended lunch with the confidence that you have helped illuminate an issue that the coworker in question should really address. After all, we are all human beings, here to help one another, right?

Fun Ways to Slack Off on the Internet

▲ Set an outrageous budget and shop for international real estate you could never afford.

▲ Google all of your friends, enemies, and coworkers.

▲ Look up the definitions of words you've never understood.

▲ Research some distant land where you would love to go on holiday regardless of whether it's feasible or not.

▲ Post heartfelt comments or vote on sites about which you are entirely uninformed.

The Colorful World of Emoticons

DID YOU KNOW?

Cyberphobia is an irrational fear of or aversion to computers and the learning of new technologies.

Logizomechanophobia is a fear specifically of computers that causes a crippling sense of helplessness and a desire to run away.

Technophobia is a fear of all modern technology, causing sufferers to avoid computers, ATMs, and the like.

Shoddy and minimal research has revealed to this author that the universally shared "smiley" emoticon was originally copyrighted by one Stephen R. Cohen sometime in the mid-eighties. While this may or may not be true, how this man might actually profit from such clairvoyance remains a mystery. In any case you won't see that little doo-hickey reproduced here for fear of a lawsuit. Instead, let us focus on some of the more entertaining variations on the smiley face that have become commonplace:

;-)............................. *I'm winking*
:-o .... *I'm surprised*
:-P............................. *I screwed up*
0:-) .... *I'm an angel*
>:-) .... *I'm a devil*
>:-I .... *I'm angry*

Can you feel the coma coming on? The lack of inspiration is crippling. But for those who require greater expression, there are a number of more colorful emoticons available that have organically evolved to express the full range of cyber-emotions that we all feel. For example:

DID YOU KNOW?

The first e-mail on record was sent out by one Ray Tomlinson in 1971. But in order to designate his intended target, he had to find a unique symbol not found in people's names, so he decided to use the now ubiquitous @ symbol.

:-(*)	*I'm about to vomit*
%-\	*I'm hungover*
|-O	*I'm yawning/snoring*
%-6	*I'm braindead*
:-). . . .	*I'm drooling*
:-Q	*I'm smoking*
| ^ o	*I'm snoring*
<:3	*Rat*
8 ^	*Chicken*
:= |	*Baboon*
<=8:-)	*Dickhead*
(./\.)	*Saggy boobs*
(o Y o)	*Big boobs*
<XXXXXX####	*I'm smoking a joint*
(_!_)	*Asshole*
(__!__)	*Fat ass*
(!)	*Tight ass*
(_*_)	*Sore ass*
(_x_)	*Kiss my ass*
(_zzz_)	*Tired ass*
(_E=mc2_)	*Smart ass*
(_?_)	*Dumb ass*
[_!_]	*Hard ass*
-->0	*Fuck You*
0<--	*Fuck Me*

Society does evolve in amusing ways, doesn't it? Cyber-speak has been distilled to the degree that human emotions, be they harmless or volatile, can be communicated in a series of simplified symbols that are sure to baffle scientists of future generations as they try to unravel the mysteries of our complex society after all has been annihilated and only a few printouts remain. These are the hieroglyphs of the electronic age.

Perils and Pitfalls

Surely, our feather-penned forefathers would be shocked and baffled by the newfangled means of communication we all now take for granted. The hand-written letter is now a relic to be marveled at in museums, and even the elderly are frantically poking and clawing at their newly purchased keyboards and other electronic gizmos in fear of being left behind. But for the modern corporate employee the medium of e-mail can be treacherous and full of potential disaster, and must therefore be negotiated with great caution. Certain rules of thumb apply. One cannot embrace modern technology with abandon. No, no, no. Restraint is everything in this new world lest we shoot our selves in the foot.

E-mail and instant messaging can wreak absolute havoc if not properly managed. Let us review the rules of workplace reserve:

Never send an angry e-mail: When heightened emotions are involved wait at least two hours before sending. Save the e-mail and reread it when your volatile emotions have settled.

Avoid impulse: Address all angry or delicate e-mails to yourself so that if you accidentally hit "send," you will not destroy an otherwise manageable relationship. When you decide that you do want to send, that is when you insert the correct screen names.

Wait it out: On endlessly long chains with multiple recipients, avoid responding as long as possible. Nine times out of ten, these tend to resolve themselves.

Think it through: By taking your time to compose a thorough communication that addresses a variety of questions or concerns you can avoid sending multiple follow-ups with every additional thought you have. Countless e-mails on the same subject make you seem disorganized and unprofessional.

Use diplomacy: Always acknowledge the positives before ripping into the negatives. A balanced perspective is essential if any change is to be effected.

CC selectively: Tattling in the workplace wreaks more revenge than benefits, so do not carbon copy with malicious intent unless you are prepared to start a war. (Of course, the blind CC is always handy when you're feeling particularly shady.)

Save all incriminating e-mails: Obviously, the lewd e-mails from your friends are harmless, but any sexually-charged communications from smarmy superiors are worth saving. You may never use them, but a special folder may come in handy one day.

Beware of using list-serves: Pre-arranged mailing lists that include those in higher positions should be used very sparingly. Ask yourself if you really want all of your coworkers and superiors to remember and possibly save this e-mail.

Ten Signs You May Be Suffering from E-mailoholism

Sure, it sounds ridiculous, but think about it. Aren't most addictions simply ways of self-medicating, suppressing, or dealing with our inabilities to connect with others or to feel excitement in a healthy and natural way? Isn't an addiction a crutch we use to compensate for an emotional void of some sort? You know it is.

In the modern office workplace e-mail is an essential part of business that requires swift

and sometimes immediate responses. That's a given. But has that knee-jerk reaction to instant communication begun to infiltrate your personal life? Is it time to reflect upon your obsessive personal habits? Just as there is a thin line between love and hate, there is a thin line between work and play. Have you crossed the line? Remember that as far as addictions go, e-mail is immediate, it holds endless possibility, and it's free! So, watch out. You may already be an e-junky and not even know it. Be honest. Do you have any of these symptoms?:

▲ You know all your friends' e-mail addresses by heart, but you don't know any of their phone numbers.

▲ You remain online even when you are not using your computer because you don't want to miss any incoming messages.

▲ You physically react and sit up straight when you hear the sound that indicates a new e-mail has arrived.

▲ You are filled with horror by the idea of not checking your personal e-mail for three days.

▲ You have ongoing e-mail relationships with people you've never met in person.

▲ You are unable to leave incoming messages unopened for twenty-four hours.

▲ You actually sit in front of your computer waiting for a response after you send an e-mail.

▲ You offer up your e-mail address rather than your phone number when you meet a new friend or a romantic prospect.

▲ You have compartmentalized your life by various screen names outside of work.

▲ You are saving e-mails between yourself and your friends because you are convinced that one day they will make a fantastic and interesting book.

I know, it's a harsh line of questioning, but no one can help you if you aren't willing to admit you have a problem. Turn off the computer and give it some thought. We're all here for you.

More New Lingo

As interoffice communications evolve, so does the vernacular that accompanies it. One must always remain abreast of the latest lingo:

DIAPER CHANGE: A visit by a member of tech support to clean up the mess you've created in your computer.

DRAILING: The act of sending a regrettable or humiliating e-mail while in a thoroughly drunken state.

NASTYGRAM: An e-mail sent to humiliate, threaten, intimidate, insult, or upset. It may be overt or subtle.

OHNOSECOND: That horrible, fleeting moment when one realizes an incriminating e-mail or instant message has been sent to the wrong person.

SWIRL CYCLE: A lengthy chain of e-mails regarding an imagined emergency that eventually fizzles out.

A SPECIAL PLACE IN HELL . . .

. . . is reserved for the idiot with the supremely annoying signature quote reading "A stranger is a friend you haven't met yet."

At the End of the Day

Never forget that your enemies may be saving your hostile diatribes. It is always best to err on the side of diplomacy and caution in workplace communications. Resist the temptation to be impulsive, and always cover your ass by remembering that e-mails can, and more often than not will, be saved, <=8:-).

Mandatory Fun

"Only two things are
infinite, the universe and
human stupidity, and I'm
not sure about the former."
>>> Albert Einstein

Hope You Can Make It!

LAUGHTER, IN ITS TRUE FORM, IS AN involuntary response to the unexpected. It is a natural, spontaneous reaction experienced when tension is built and then released by a humorous surprise. That is why we laugh when someone slips and falls into a snow bank. We didn't see it coming, and neither did they. If we can see the punch line coming, the comedy is lost. The same holds true of enjoyment and fun in general. The enjoyment is rooted in spontaneity. If the good times are scheduled to begin at 5 p.m. and end promptly at 6 p.m., chances are the "fun" won't be all that much . . . fun.

One of the unintentionally comical aspects of corporate office life is the persistently held and doggedly pursued belief that such things can be manufactured. Though the directive usually comes in the form of an innocent invitation, the meaning is always clear. Fun has been scheduled. Attendance is optional, but absence is always noted. The invitations are presented as a gesture of good will, entirely devoid of ulterior motives. Your multi-billion dollar corporation has decided, purely out of warm, fuzzy feelings, to pick up that $300 bar tab! This is what is known in the corporate world as "mandatory fun."

While the forms in which mandatory fun may be prescribed are many, forced social situations intended to foster team spirit and camaraderie are usually so transparent and manipulative that they rarely result in the intended effect. This should not be particularly surprising, but the struggle against the obvious persists relentlessly. Inevitably, most of us find ourselves regularly shepherded off to excruciating events designed to achieve the impossible. We all see right through them, but we play along so as to avoid being pegged as the employee with the bad attitude. It's an inescapable part of corporate life, and you are powerless to resist, so you may as well just think of it all as an opportunity to hone your acting chops. Herewith, a review of the most vexing:

PEP RALLIES

We've all seen video footage of maniacally grinning corporate employees gathered together in auditoriums, or even stadiums, clapping, chanting, and cheering to show their team spirit and dedication to the corporation. And while it is both amusing and disturbing to witness such cult-like devotion, it is even more amazing to think that there are large numbers of limp-minded individuals who can actually be so easily led. If you ever have the misfortune to find yourself in the midst of such a dispiriting display, simply lock eyes with the nearest sane person and hold on for dear life. Suppress your giggles, resist the giddy euphoria, clap along, and get the hell out of there. Under no circumstances should you ever agree to attend any après-events, because that is where the real brainwashing kicks in.

HAPPY HOUR

While a happy hour spent with friends can be very enjoyable indeed, a forced ordeal in which management invites "team members" to get together for a jovial evening of cocktails is rarely a happy experience. The lucky among us who actually like every one of their coworkers may feel differently, but for most of us there are at least one or two coworkers with whom we would never want to be caught dead in public. In such situations it is imperative to identify your allies early on and form a tight clique with a strong force field around you. Create a close circle, avoid eye contact with the dreaded ones, and do not let the conversation lag for even a moment, for that is precisely when the office drip will wander up and murmur, "Hey guys, how's it going?" Then you're screwed.

HOLIDAY PARTIES

Depending upon your place of employment, these may be lavish affairs with big budgets, a tragic cluster of employees in a cafeteria festooned with crepe paper, or anything in between. But regardless of the scale, certain inevitable scenarios will likely arise. There will be the shy, barely notice-able employee who becomes loudly shit-faced, the girl who ends up in tears because she lost her purse, the unlikely couple that steals off for some messy snogging, and the supremely unappealing employee who decides that this is the time to sidle up to you, bleary-eyed and red-faced, to make a pass. Throw in a couple of guys from sales who decide to wrestle and a handful of executives who decide to reveal their inner funk by dirty dancing, and you've got yourself a holiday party.

This
is
Hell

SECRET SANTA

This would be the torturous office tradition in which each employee is forced to take time out during the busy holiday season to brave the crowds at Barnes & Noble or Virgin Records only to stand in line to buy a ten-dollar gift certificate for that irritating ass down the hall who you're not all that crazy about to begin with. With the odds always stacked against you, you are likely to be rewarded for your efforts with some utterly useless item that you have to drag around all evening so you don't leave it behind and hurt your Secret Santa's feelings. Depending upon how highly you are esteemed by your holiday stalker, your lovely prize might be an empty frame with a slogan on it, a cheap acrylic sweater in the wrong size, a mean-spirited choice of a book that addresses your "issues," or a gag sex toy over which you must feign shock and surprise. Of course, the good thing about getting a sex toy is that all the drunks will want to play with it so you can just claim that it was stolen.

OFFICE BIRTHDAY PARTIES

This is, of course, a misguided use of the term "party." Office birthday parties usually involve little more than the perkiest of employees banding together to ambush an unsuspecting victim quietly tending to their business with a cake. As the singing begins, the prairie dog effect kicks in and soon everyone is standing around the red-faced employee who remains seated with a frozen smile. When the song ends there is usually a smattering of applause and the victim weakly tells his or her coworkers how nice they are. Then everyone realizes the forks and knives are in the kitchen so the sad procession back begins. Everyone chats and chews until just enough time has elapsed so that they may leave without seeming rude. Joyous.

THE BOSS'S BARBECUE

Woe to those who actually get invited to the boss's home for an afternoon barbecue. Beyond the horror of seeing one's boss in cargo shorts, there are countless other awkward situations to be navigated. Take for example the fact that this is the time when employees will often decide to trot out their children. And while your own children and those of your friends may be adorable—and of course they are—there is a simple law of the universe that dictates that if you don't like the parents, you're not going to like their hideous offspring. So, the married people mingle, the nonemployee spouses hover patiently, the single people huddle together while everyone gets mildly sunburned.

DID YOU KNOW?

Prozac is the most widely used antidepressant in the world.

GOING AWAY PARTIES

If a friend of yours is leaving the company, chances are you will arrange on your own for a nice dinner or evening of cocktails with that person and a close group of friends from the office. This is perfectly reasonable. However, when the boss announces that the wildly annoying coworker with the gray tooth and the bad attitude is leaving and "we're all going to Charlie's Tavern to send him off," it is often difficult to get out of the dreaded affair. Invariably the boss and the unpopular employee arrive first as everyone else is competing to arrive last. Once fortified with a drink or two, every employee is obligated to approach the departee and lob out some gem along the lines of "I can't believe it," or "Good for you," or, worst of all, "So how does it feel?" Inevitably, after the cocktails have been flowing, some drunken fool will blurt

"A conference is a gathering of important people who singly can do nothing, but together can decide that nothing can be done."
>>> Fred Allen

out: "I'm SO going to miss you!" That's when everyone else exchanges furtive glances and starts heading for the door. In the end, everyone feels dirty.

OUT-OF-TOWN CONFERENCES

The most grueling of all corporate experiences is the out-of-town conference, during which "mixers" and/or "fun nights" have been planned. To be fair, these can actually be quite humorous and entertaining depending upon the crowd, but there are red flags to watch for. The first among these is the presence of an unusually perky "event planner." You'll know whether or not you're in trouble when you stop by the greeting table to get your name tag. Excessive instructions, kooky questionnaires, color-coding of any kind, and any mention of comfortable shoes should all set off bells and be met with suspicion. If you hear the words "games" or "teams," run. The trick as always is to seek out allies. Do everything you can to circumvent forced groupings. Trade that yellow balloon for a green one, switch numbers, or rearrange the place cards, just don't let them separate you from your friends or you will be very sorry indeed.

Making Mandatory Fun More Fun

Help
Help
HELP

If you are unable to escape the inevitable, there's no reason you can't have a good time and liven things up in social situations, be they forced or voluntary:

❖ In a conference situation arrive early and rearrange seating cards to suit your purposes and torment your friends.

❖ At the office happy hour send a drink to an unsuspecting target and tell the bartender it's "from the boss." Offer a big tip if they add a wink.

❖ Confidentially tell the lecherous office pervert that your enemy thinks "you don't like him."

❖ Buy the notoriously promiscuous office employee a few extra rounds.

❖ Once he or she is totally tanked, ask the boss to make a speech.

❖ Initiate the game "The Most Embarrassing Thing That Ever Happened to Me" and disappear before it's your turn.

❖ Combat the bad karma you are accumulating elsewhere by genuinely engaging the office wallflower or the perpetual sad sack in genuine conversation. After all, you are a sensitive humanitarian above all else, am I correct?

Excellent Excuses

If you are employed at all, you have certainly been ambushed with an invitation to attend some horrendous after-work soirée. A sudden invitation out of the blue can often leave you stammering for an out, but all you really need to escape the proceedings is to have a few preplanned, believable excuses up your sleeve. Of course, all excuses are best sold with a little touch of regret and disappointment.

I have plans: Painfully simple, of course, but this is the most commonly employed excuse in a pinch. The trouble often comes when you are asked what those plans might be. Trying to think something up on the spot often leads to stammering and a tendency to over-explain. Therefore, you should decide on a stock answer in advance. Once you've used "My college roommate is in town," you'll need a new one to keep in mind going forward.

I have to walk the dog: Easy to remember if, in fact, you do have a dog. No one will ever question your responsible devotion as you spin your sad tale of the lonely dog cooped up at home with an expanding bladder. Of course, this excuse is best for singles as those with live-in loves or extended families will have a harder sell, but if pressed you can always claim that they're out of town.

I have a personal appointment: The vagueness of this line will keep coworkers from probing further. Dates, grocery shopping, and random errands can always be rearranged or postponed, so it needs to be an "appointment." Even if it's early in the evening, they'll be too busy wondering if you're having an affair, seeing a shrink, or having an affair with your shrink to try and talk you out of it.

My parents are visiting from out of town: The beauty here is that everyone can empathize with this one, and so no one even thinks to question it, unless of course you recently lied and took time off to attend your parents' funeral. A knowing nod of the head and some shared rolling of eyeballs will only bring you closer to your boss as you blow him or her off.

I have a seriously upset stomach: With proper emphasis on the word "seriously," this little number will conjure up all sorts of ugly imagery and will not likely be questioned. An additional benefit is that you will be admired for your forthright and candid confession. Be sure to walk strangely as you depart for maximum impact.

In the event that an invitation is extended several days or even weeks in advance, an entirely different and far more creative set of excuses would be in order. Be sure you are prepared.

I have tickets to the theater that night: Claims of having tickets to a concert or a sporting event are always risky as specific dates can be checked and often change. Make sure you are always aware of at least one ongoing show that has been running forever.

That's my kid/wife/husband/girlfriend/boyfriend's birthday: A nice blanket excuse if in fact you have any of the above. Hopefully, the person inviting you out does not know the person about whom you are lying, as this may lead to awkward trip-ups. If this is the case, jump to a tangential relationship such as my wife's father, my boyfriend's brother, etc.

I have a class that night: Be prepared to follow up with a plausible tale of what inspired you to secretly sign up for a pottery class, Tae Kwon Do, or French lessons. Bear in mind that a limited series of classes in a mundane category requires less story maintenance, though you will have to be unavailable on that same night for at least a few weeks, so get your story straight.

I think that may be the day after my operation: Obviously, this excuse requires back-up lies and should only be employed if you are willing to schedule a few vacation days to secure the ruse. Foot operations, mild hernias, or "personal" operations are the most believable and easily played off. If you are not blessed with theatrical skills, you can always pin the operation on your significant other and bemoan the burden of it all.

I would rather eat tin foil: Well, sometimes you just have to tell it like it is.

DID YOU KNOW?

The term "happy hour" originated in the U.S. Navy during the 1920s. It referred to on-ship performances in which the performers were usually drunk.

So, What Really Is Fun in the Workplace?

Well, a lot actually. It's only the bad ideas that are forced upon us that ruffle our collective feathers, so let's not paint too gloomy a picture here. Even in the most tiresome of jobs good friends and a good attitude can go a long way. It's important to separate the drudgery of work from the pleasures to be found in good company.

> "Work is the refuge of people who have nothing better to do."
> >>> Oscar Wilde

While we all moan and groan about having to go to work week after week, there's something to be said for having someplace to go every day, and having a group of people you actually look forward to seeing each day, even if the work itself is a drag. If you're lucky enough to have friends in your place of employment, you're very lucky. As you stagger around getting ready in the morning, think about looking forward to seeing them rather than obsessing about all the things on your to-do list.

In a highly stressful atmosphere where constant changes and constant demands for more can be very exhausting, the time you spend socializing—even if it is only for a few moments—is extremely valuable and can really humanize the workplace. So, don't think of your social time as stolen moments or something to get away with, think of it as part of the job and allow yourself to slow down and enjoy your convivial interactions. There is no report so urgent that it can't wait five minutes while you catch up on social matters.

So, even though mandatory fun may be inescapable from time to time, you have every right to enjoy your day and there are ample opportunities to liven up that day. Depending on how agreeable the boss is, see if you can work some genuine fun into the work week:

TRASHY MOVIE DAY: If the boss will "sign off" on the idea, get the whole staff together and leave the office once a month to catch an afternoon matinee. The dumber the movie the better.

A PICNIC IN THE PARK: Though it may not be practical on a daily basis, those rare and spectacularly beautiful days must be taken advantage of. When they come along make arrangements immediately to get out of the office and enjoy, even if only briefly.

MIDDAY SHOPPING: If you do have an hour allotted to you, and you're not sequestered away in some isolated, corporate compound in the woods, use that time to go to a bookstore or go out and buy something for yourself. You can always keep typing while you have your sandwich back at the desk.

POST-WORK DRINKS AND DINING: Replace those awful holiday party memories with regular nights out with the people you actually like. Make it a point to go out for cocktails or dinner on a semi-regular basis to ensure that your relationships aren't entirely based upon work.

GUILTY PLEASURE TELEVISION: Have you discovered that your friends all enjoy the same stupid show you're addicted to? Rather than just having rushed discussions about it in the kitchen, make a point of getting together each week at someone's place to make it a weekly party.

JOIN THE SPORTS TEAMS: If you actually enjoy the sport in question and none of your arch enemies are on the team, why not grab a friend and sign up if you think it might be a laugh. You might even meet some new friends or get to meet that hottie from the other department.

The underlying message here is not to let the mandatory office fun become the only social outlet you have at work. If you don't take the bull by the horns and schedule something on your own now and then, you really can't complain too much. And you'll find that those God-awful forced get-togethers become a lot less God-awful when you actually have some good times mixed in.

There is, of course, one other thing that falls under the category of "workplace fun," but it's a big gamble and a potentially dangerous game. And that's why it requires a whole chapter unto itself.

CHAPTER

9

Sex
in the
Workplace

"Anything worth doing
is worth doing slowly."
>>> Mae West

Consider the Odds

THE CURRENT SIZE OF THE GLOBAL workforce is nothing short of staggering. On a daily basis billions of people swarm into and out of high-rise office buildings, corporate compounds, and local branches of larger companies. Many people spend more time each week with their coworkers than their families or friends. A variety of relationships are established in the workplace, new friendships form, flirtations occur, and happy hours fuel the libidos of corporate employees desperate for some sense of life in a seemingly meaningless atmosphere of boredom. This can only mean one thing: There's an awful lot of boinking going on in and out of the office.

Despite the best efforts of corporations and companies to discourage interoffice relations, a quick peek at the statistics would suggest that the inevitable is . . . well, inevitable. Here is the breakdown on the sex divide in 2003, according to the International Labour Organisation:

COUNTRY	MALE WORKERS	FEMALE WORKERS
United States	73.33 million	64.40 million
Japan	32.35 million	25.97 million
Germany	20.00 million	15.57 million
Italy	13.81 million	5.34 million
United Kingdom	13.77 million	8.89 million
France	13.43 million	7.73 million
Canada	6.76 million	4.98 million

When presented with such numbers, one begins to wonder. Though many may be married or in committed cohabitations, it would be naïve to calculate the potential numbers of hook-ups based on such criteria. Forbidden romances, various sexual orientations, and modern sexual attitudes in general defy all such trivial details. You just never know.

The very limited table above accounts for more than 300 million workers in a mere seven countries. A simple mathematical equation calculating the number of potential hook-ups clearly reveals that . . . well, math can be tricky, but . . . hey, there are probably more than a few people in your workplace who are getting it on!

Truth be told, most of us are too numbed by our jobs to bother with judgment. We just want to know the gossip. It's fun to stumble upon a clandestine romance. We want to know who's doing whom, how long it's been going on, and, God please, let there be scandalous details!

It's only human nature. Of course, if you happen to be among those involved in an office romance, it would behoove you from the get-go to bear in mind that the vultures are craning their necks, looking for clues, and eager to spread the news. And don't kid yourself. You will be found out.

"Sex between a man and a woman can be absolutely wonderful—provided you get between the right man and the right woman."
>>> Woody Allen

Still, the thrilling allure of a workplace romance is hard to resist. The danger, the secrecy, and the stolen moments can be intoxicating. What better way to add excitement to an otherwise dull routine? Unfortunately, in the highly regimented, closely monitored, PC world in which we live, your unbridled lust may have consequences. These might include:

❖ Legal problems

❖ Public embarrassment

❖ Accusations of favoritism

❖ Sexual harassment charges

❖ A damaged reputation

❖ Crabs

Of course, such trivial matters rarely cross our minds when we are faced with the thrilling prospect of an exciting, lurid, tawdry, or forbidden affair.

The Facts

According to Vault's 2005 Office Romance Survey, 58 percent of the office workers polled admitted that they have been involved in an office romance, 31 percent said that they had not, and 11 percent said they had not, but they would be willing to if the opportunity arose. The findings in general reflected a fairly open-minded attitude toward romance in the work place. Here are a few more statistics:

▲ 14 percent of the respondents had dated a boss.

▲ 19 percent had dated a subordinate.

▲ 23 percent admitted to having trysts within the office walls.

▲ 22 percent reported that their office romances resulted in marriage or long-term relationships.

▲ 32 percent of the respondents tried to hide their relationships, but were found out.

▲ 26 percent claimed to have successfully concealed their relationship from everyone.

▲ 59 percent felt that office romances were not a big deal.

Additionally, the survey showed that certain industries were perceived to be more conducive than others to the old slap and tickle. Respondents felt that the media/entertainment field was the ripest for happy hook-ups, followed by the fields of advertising, marketing, and consulting. The least likely candidates for interoffice interplay were thought to be those involved in financial or technological industries.

OFFICE
SUPPLY
ROOM, 5:30.
LOSE THE
PANTIES.

Perception, however, does not necessarily reflect reality, so don't be too sure that your accountant or the IT tech down the hall aren't having it off.

Sex, Lies, and Romance

Does your company have a policy regarding romance in the workplace? You might be surprised. While some large corporations have fairly liberal policies, others have strict policies on interoffice dating and romance that fall into one of two categories. The first of these is the antinepotism policy, which is based on the idea that professional advancement may be affected by a personal relationship between two employees. Sometimes a mere change of department is enough in such cases to get around any possible problems.

The second type of policy is one of nonfraternization, which is based on the idea that personal relationships between employees can interrupt workflow, create conflicts of interest, or bring about a negative work environment. Of course, the biggest concern of the employers is that, if the relationship tanks, the door swings wide open for sexual harassment lawsuits if the disgruntled ex-lovers decide to torment one another.

The truth is that the lower you are on the totem pole, the less likely it is that your office romance will be the cause of any great concern. After all, nobody cares who the powerless are sleeping with. It's those who have influence that are under the greatest scrutiny.

In any case, regardless of the office policy or lack thereof, the most important thing about workplace romances is that they provide endless entertainment for the rest of us. Whose toes wouldn't curl in delight upon discovering that two of your coworkers have been getting it on? Of course, a secret affair that is successfully concealed is of no use to anyone, so it pays to be a good detective. You have to watch for the signs if you're going to get any enjoyment at all out of your slutty coworkers' escapades.

TELL-TALE SIGNS THAT YOUR COWORKERS ARE GETTING IT ON

* The two suspects rigidly avoid all eye contact in conference rooms or meetings of any kind.

* You spot one of the suspects waiting around inexplicably on the sidewalk or in the parking lot.

* The suspects happen to schedule long weekends or time off from work concurrently.

DID YOU KNOW?

WATCH OUT!
It is estimated that 11,000 Americans injure themselves each year by trying out new and unusual sexual positions.

DID YOU KNOW?

BUSY BODIES

According to the World Health Organization, approximately 100 million acts of sexual intercourse take place each day.

❖ A suddenly self-conscious formality exists between the suspects as they interact in the workplace.

❖ One or both of the suspects suddenly exhibits a change in style more closely aligned with that of the other. (Watch for new haircuts, sexier clothing, etc.)

❖ Rapid weight loss and/or suspicious glow in either of the two parties due to excessive bunny sex.

❖ Curiously simultaneous arrivals to the office and synchronized departures.

❖ Whispered conversations that when interrupted suddenly become very vague and jovial.

Any one of these signs on its own may not be proof of an ongoing tryst, but the more signs you see, the more likely it is that you're really onto something. Of course, as with all things shallow and superficial, voyeurism gets old after a while. And that's when it's time to consider whipping up some frisky business of your own.

Tips for the Tawdry

Should you find yourself to be the one in bed with a coworker, you must be careful not to exhibit any of the revealing clues listed above. Additionally, there are certain guidelines to keep in mind to prevent your little dalliance from descending into unnecessary drama.

▲ Make sure you're both on the same page as to whether it's a onetime hook-up you're dealing with or something more.

▲ Remember that office discretion and workplace policies are excellent excuses to keep things from going any further.

▲ Understand from the very beginning that other coworkers will almost surely find you out.

▲ Do not reveal any extreme fetishes, kinky secrets, or humiliating shortcomings that you don't want revealed to the whole office.

▲ At all costs, avoid messy breakups or cruel snubs. It's not as if you can avoid the other person after you've callously dumped them.

POPULAR HOT SPOTS FOR QUICK ACTION

Sometimes, lust simply refuses to be stifled, and certain locations in and around the office are ideal for a quick grope or a stolen moment. Keep these fun spots in mind for your own bouts of unbridled passion. On the other hand, if you're hot on the trail of two

lusty cohorts, these are the places to monitor most closely:

- ❖ A private office
- ❖ A bathroom
- ❖ A conference room
- ❖ A stairwell
- ❖ An elevator
- ❖ The copy room
- ❖ A closet
- ❖ The kitchen
- ❖ The parking lot

New Lingo

Sex in the workplace is always treacherous and potentially dangerous, but there are certain stereotypes that tend to add an extra dimension of complication to an office hook-up. Use extra caution when dealing with:

THE HASBIAN: A lesbian who suddenly switches gears and becomes involved in a hetero-sexual relationship.

THE HETEROFLEXIBLE: A straight person whom

you suspect might be open to experimentation after three or ten beers.

THE BATMOBILER: One who has an arsenal of easily accessed defenses to be employed in the face of intimacy.

THE KOALA CLINGER: A lover who instantly latches on as a Koala Bear to a eucalyptus tree.

THE DRUNK DIALER: That person who has a tendency to make cloying, tearful, or needy phone calls when inebriated.

THE PITY SHAG: Always available at office drink-ups, this is perhaps the most regrettable of all copulations as it requires the most intricate and creative of escapes.

THE CLIMBER BOINK: Whether you are the one climbing or the target of the climb, the embarrassment of any such liaison usually sinks any hope of advancement.

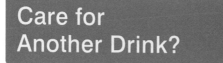

Care for Another Drink?

It should come as no surprise that many office romances are initiated in situations where alcohol is involved. Holiday parties, happy hours, and boozy business conferences held in hotels are the most likely scenarios after which coworkers may wake up next to one another in a state of post-coital shock.

Being fully aware of this obvious fact, a seasoned spy will be on his or her toes in such situations, on the lookout for tell-tale signs. Naturally, the greater the number of people and the longer the night drags on, the greater the possibilities are of stumbling upon potential scandal. A skilled sleuth always keeps an eye open for any hints of impending involvements. Watch for:

- ▲ Lingering hands on the back, the shoulder, the arm, or, most tellingly, the leg.
- ▲ Unexpected pairings in which the two suspects are rarely apart.
- ▲ Relaxed body language involving touching thighs or unusual closeness.
- ▲ Simultaneous drinking speeds and synchronized rounds.
- ▲ Flashes of meaningful eye contact.
- ▲ Excessive hair flipping.
- ▲ Humorously model-like posing.
- ▲ Confidential whispers.
- ▲ A simultaneous departure.

Then again, you may be the one throwing off signs left and right as you plot and scheme to have your way with your hottie in question. And, truth be told, it's pretty hard to set up a liaison without exhibiting at least a few of these standard giveaways, and so subtlety is always advisable. If you hope to keep things under wraps at all, just try not to be blatantly obvious.

YOUR BOOZY COHORTS

According to the *Journal of Studies on Alcohol:*

7 percent: American workers who drink during the workday

9 percent: Workers who have had a hangover at work

15 percent: Workers who say they've directly been affected by alcohol at work

14 million: Estimated number of Americans who abuse alcohol or are alcoholics

The Prelude to Your Walk of Shame

So, the deed has been done, you spent the night and there you are between the sheets as the

Guzzle
and/or
Chug

sun pours into the room. Your head feels like it weighs ninety pounds and your mouth feels like you've swallowed a sock. Now what? Before you begin the proverbial "walk of shame" back to your hotel room or out of the building, your first course of action is crucial in determining the aftermath of your affair.

Regardless of whether it turns out to be a one-night-stand or an ongoing relationship there are several options to be considered upon awakening, and each one has its own set of pros and cons:

THE SILENT ESCAPE

This one involves great stealth as you gather your belongings, get dressed, and silently flee the scene without waking the other person.

UPSIDE: Depending on the amount of alcohol consumed the night before, the entire debacle could be forgotten or written off as a bad dream.

DOWNSIDE: Your swift departure may be considered an inexcusable insult and result in an eventual confrontation.

THE HAND-WRITTEN NOTE

Far more polite than the silent escape, a considerate and/or humorous note left behind for your sleeping friend is an acknowledgement without commitment.

UPSIDE: "Didn't want to wake you . . ." implies a certain level of concern and respect after a tawdry romp and will hopefully keep things civil between you.

DOWNSIDE: A written message usually results in a response of some sort. By acknowledging the deed you will have to address the situation at some point.

THE MORNING DISCUSSION

Usually an awkward situation at best, this provides the opportunity to set the tone of expectations. In general, references to the past ("Wow, we sure drank a LOT!") indicate regret, while references to the future ("I'll call you tonight.") indicate hope.

UPSIDE: A mature evaluation of the situation will hopefully clear the air and leave no hard feelings.

DOWNSIDE: This may be the point where you both discover that you feel very differently about what happened.

MORNING SEX

An enthusiastic second go-round is a fairly good indication that both parties are fairly pleased with the evening's outcome. Then again, having sex in broad daylight and with a headache can lead to serious reevaluation.

UPSIDE: You get to have sex twice in a very short period of time and, at the very least, you both can rest assured that neither of you considers it all a horrible mistake.

DOWNSIDE: In most cases morning sex carries with it the implication that this will likely be an ongoing thing. So, always think twice before you shag twice.

Interoffice romance is always tricky business. Whether you're the subject of the scandal or the devious detective, it's always important to remember that there may actually be genuine feelings involved. And though it's true that sensitivity may dampen the fun for all involved, it never hurts to err on the side of discretion. So, before you set the gossip mill in motion, consider the fact that you may one day require a little bit of understanding and sympathy after an ill-advised coupling of your own.

CHAPTER

10

Preserving Your Soul in a Soulless Business World

"One of the symptoms
of an approaching nervous
breakdown is the belief
that one's work is
terribly important."
>>> Bertrand Russell

Just Breathe

ACCORDING TO THE 2000 ANNUAL "ATTITUDES in the American Workplace VI" Gallup Poll, 80 percent of workers reported that they feel stress on the job, 25 percent said they have felt like screaming or shouting at work, and 9 percent reported that they were aware of an assault or violent act in their place of work. Numbers such as these clearly reveal that a whole lot of people are taking their work far too seriously.

Though stress can be imposed upon us by tyrannical bosses, unrealistic demands, or impossible deadlines, it is still our responsibility to manage and control the extent to which that stress affects us. After all, it's not just a question of mood.

- ❖ Stress can contribute to heart disease, high blood pressure, strokes, and other illnesses.

- ❖ Stress also affects the immune system, leaving you more susceptible to disease and illness.

- ❖ Stress is often a contributing factor in the development of alcoholism, obesity, suicide, drug addiction, and cigarette addiction.

- ❖ Stress can turn even the most beautiful face into something resembling a cat's asshole.

The simple fact is that stress is an actual physical reaction to a perceived danger or threat. In times of great stress the deeply rooted animal fight-or-flight instinct kicks in and your whole body goes into upheaval. Steroid hormones and adrenaline are released, heart rate and blood pressure are both increased, breathing becomes more rapid, and blood flow is diverted. That's a lot of internal chaos, and chronic stress only magnifies the situation as the body attempts to suppress the chemical typhoon within.

If you're going to have any hope at all of preserving your soul, you must first gain control of your stress levels. It is worth remembering that stress and its symptoms are based on reaction. And reaction is based on perceptions, which in turn are based on thoughts. Hence, in order to nip the problem in the bud, you need to control your thoughts. Unless you're performing brain surgery or launching the space shuttle, chances are your work does not have life or death consequences, so when the evil demons begin to swirl inside, stop and take a moment to step back and calm down.

▲ Resist being pulled into the drama that surrounds you.

▲ Remember that you can work faster and more effectively if you remain calm.

DID YOU KNOW?

According to The American Institute for Stress, repetitive musculoskeletal injuries like carpal tunnel syndrome have become the nation's leading workplace health cost and account for almost a third of all workers' compensation awards.

▲ Remind yourself that no one's life is at stake.

▲ Look out the window to remind yourself that there is life outside of your office.

▲ Be proactive in helping others to calm down.

▲ Don't take things personally in working situations.

▲ Take a breath, shrug your shoulders, and then release.

▲ Picture yourself beside a pool sipping a cocktail in a tropical setting.

▲ Picture the maniac who is aggravating you being hauled off in a straight jacket.

Avoiding Somnolence

Stress is but one affliction among many that may be having an adverse effect on your quality of life. If you regularly find yourself irritable, aggravated, and unable to concentrate at work, it may be stress-related. Then again, you may just have a serious drinking problem. But if neither of these is the case, it may just be persistent somnolence, which is a state of drowsiness caused by sleep deprivation. It is said that the average human brain is wired to withstand about sixteen hours of "wakefulness." Beyond that, alertness, reaction time, judgment, and mood can all begin a slippery slide downhill.

Sleep, in and of itself, is one of life's most appealing features, yet many of us deprive ourselves of the generally-accepted-to-be-healthy eight hours. The fact is that the time you spend drooling into your pillow is time well spent. Though your dreams may find you in Times Square in your underpants, which is admittedly stressful, your brain is actually consolidating memory, processing data, and restoring your ability to judge, learn, and solve problems. Sleep deprivation results in lack of focus, foul moods, and embarrassing bouts of narcolepsy.

So, before you blame the tedious meeting, the warm room temperature, or your horrible, stressful "work dreams" for causing you to nod off at work, you need to make some adjustments at home. The point of getting sufficient sleep at night is not to make you more productive at work so much as it is to make you more efficient at work. With a clear head you will be able to complete your tasks more quickly and painlessly, thus allowing you more time for multislacking and socializing with your preferred coworkers.

"Disbelief in magic can force a poor soul into believing in government and business."
>>> Tom Robbins

> "A great
> secret of
> success
> is to go
> through life
> as a man who
> never gets
> used up."
> >>> Albert
> Schweitzer

The temptation to stay up late is often fueled by a desperate attempt to fend off the 'morrow and maximize one's downtime as if the dreaded job did not exist. Unfortunately, this plan is self-defeating. The world keeps turning and the morning always comes. That horrible feeling, as you hit the snooze button for the eleventh time, loving your sheets yet knowing you are running late, can be alleviated. It merely takes a little self-discipline:

Don't watch TV in bed: Deny it though you may, you know you are powerless in the face of that "I Dream of Jeannie" marathon.

Don't oversleep on weekends: You're not really catching up. It only throws off your biological clock making Monday even more miserable.

Don't eat late at night: It's that turbulent digestion process that is giving you those horrible work nightmares in which you can't catch up.

Drink early: If you're having cocktails on a week night, begin in the early evening. If you drink too much, your sleep may be somewhat impaired, but at least you'll be conked out by eleven.

Cut to the chase: If you know you're going to be having sex on a week night, dispense with the long buildup and just do it. The earlier you exhaust yourself, the better.

Read a book: Admit it. Your attention span isn't what it once was. Mindless late-night television can drag you along indefinitely, but reading takes concentration and is therefore a much better barometer of when you are truly spent.

Keeping the Zen

As was previously stated, unless you are a brain surgeon (in which case I cannot be held legally liable for any of the advice proffered in this book because I was only kidding), you simply can't take your work too seriously. You need to show up, you need to deliver, and you need to respect the work and responsibilities for which you are being paid. But, really, there's no need to work yourself into a frenzy.

For the emotionally sensitive the workplace can be a very treacherous minefield. There are those among us who actually absorb the emotional states, the anxieties, and the neuroses of those that surround them. If this applies to you, you must learn to delineate between other people's problems and your own. Just because your coworkers or your superiors are in a tizzy doesn't mean that you are obligated to participate in the drama. It is wise to keep abreast of the emotional landscape, but you cannot let your own emotional state be dictated by others.

Even in the face of emotional tirades, panic attacks, and utter rage, a wise and serene employee will retain his or her own sense of calm, recognizing that another person's meltdown is merely something to be scientifically observed, not something in which to participate. It is a simple question of emotional detachment. If the drawing of such borders is difficult for you, there is a simple benchmark by which you can determine whether any situation truly warrants panic. "Am I being punched in the face right now?"

Being punched in the face is a really and truly unpleasant situation that actually warrants emotional investment. Anything short of that is manageable. Really, it is very easy to be swept up in the swirl created by those around us, but it is essential to not allow oneself to be so easily manipulated. You must recognize that there are tormented souls who thrive on drama, and it is your duty to protect yourself from such chaotic drivel. Do not participate. Always remember:

- ❖ The world will not end if this doesn't go as planned.
- ❖ Calm resolve is the antidote to hysteria.
- ❖ My most extreme emotions are reserved for my life, not my job.
- ❖ The more witnesses there are to my boss's meltdown, the better my chances of advancement.
- ❖ If the ship goes down, I'll find another ship.
- ❖ My vacation is going to be truly excellent.

The author of the best-selling *The Metrosexual Guide to Style*, *The Hedonism Handbook*, and *The Fame Game*, **MICHAEL FLOCKER** lives in New York City.

Creative Outlets

Anyone who has a creative, artistic outlet outside the workplace will tell you that to deprive oneself of that creative outlet is to feel lonely. It's as if something is missing, something sad has taken hold, and oftentimes that person doesn't even realize what's wrong. If you have a talent, a passion, or even a hobby, you must respect it. To get lost in creation, whether it's music, painting, writing, wood-working, or motorcycle restoration is the very definition of Zen. Anything that makes you lose track of time because you are totally immersed in it is something to be treasured and nurtured.

It is very easy to become consumed by one's work, and in an ideal world your work would be your passion. But the truth is that most of us are merely working for survival. Do not feel guilty if your job is not your passion. You may have circumstances that require you to maintain a certain income and tangential benefits, but that doesn't mean that you should forfeit your true passion.

Sing your ass off at karaoke, start writing that novel, or knit those damn mittens. It is only when we give up on our passions that we are truly defeated. Your passions may never result in an all-consuming, multimillion-dollar career, but that

> "Formulate and stamp indelibly on your mind a mental picture of yourself as succeeding. Hold this picture tenaciously. Never permit it to fade. Your mind will seek to develop the picture . . . Do not build up obstacles in your imagination."
> >>> Norman Vincent Peale

DID YOU KNOW?

Half the world—nearly three billion people—live on less than two dollars a day.

(source: Globalissues.org)

is not the goal. The goal is to have a balanced life. Whether it's your kids, your art, your triathlon, or your plans to travel the world one day, you must have something of value—something that is yours—to look forward to outside of work.

Even the most psychotic workaholic needs an alternative. Even if you are fortunate enough to genuinely love your work, you need something else, if only to provide balance. It may be family, friends, adventure, romance, or any form of art. But you need to have a life beyond the office. After all, those waves of depression and those feelings of hopelessness all come from the same place, and that is the belief that your job is all you have and all you ever will have. And if you believe that, then you become even more dependent upon the job, which in turn reinforces your resentments. And that, my friend, really is depressing. It is also a false assumption.

To live in fear of failure or to obsess about the possibility of being laid off is energy wasted. Throughout history people have survived far worse, and they always will. We all become attached to our lifestyles and our material things, but the truth is that all of that is temporary. If the house burns down, it burns down and you just have to keep going. Life is never short of surprises, so you can never really claim to be trapped. And if worse comes to worse, you move to Jamaica and open a braiding shack on the beach. You'll find that the more you are able to address your fears and let go of them, the less gloomy your outlook will become.

You are not your job. You can walk away at any time. It may not be easy, and it may not be a wise choice at this particular time, but just keeping that in mind can be very empowering.

Remember the People of Muddy Gut Holler

At the end of the day, it's always a good idea to sit down and take a moment to reflect on one's current situation. A little dose of reality and perspective can do wonders for the soul. They say that there will always be persons greater and lesser than yourself, and that applies to all aspects of life.

Many years ago I saw a television documentary that I have never forgotten. It was about a small community of miners in an Appalachian town called, of all things, Muddy Gut Holler. And in this "holler" families lived in squalid little homes made of corrugated tin and plywood. In every home buckets captured the rain that leaked through the ceiling as the crazy-haired, exhausted women cooked gruel over open flames while their grubby little cross-eyed children sat listlessly nearby on a bare mattress staring into the camera lens.

Nearly all of the men in town worked in a decrepit old mine into which they were pulled through an eighteen-inch opening, lying on their backs on a dolly, more than a mile inside the mountain. Once inside, they worked all day long in the dark, with only a headlamp attached to their helmets, breathing toxic fumes for the lowest pay legally allowed.

At one point in the documentary the camera focused in on a truly ancient-looking, scrawny little man. His deeply wrinkled face was black with soot and his stooped posture spoke volumes about his health and the harshness of his existence as he hobbled his way along the winding dirt road that he followed every day to return to his toothless family on the hill.

The narrator's voice kicked in. "This is Earl, and he has been working in the mines since he was thirteen years old. He is currently suffering from advanced emphysema and is quickly losing his eyesight after decades of working in the darkness of the mine. Even if he could find transportation to the nearest hospital, which is more than a hundred miles away, he could not afford to pay for the treatment his ailments require. Earl is forty-two."

To this day I can still see Earl shuffling along the dirt road, and every time I think of him, my own problems miraculously evaporate on the spot. It is very easy to sink into a state of self-pity when we become bored, complacent, or dispirited, but perspective has a way of drawing out the real truth in any situation. So the next time you're slacking off at work, reading about wealthy celebrities and their fabulous lives, convincing yourself that your life is crap, remember the people of Muddy Gut Holler.

DID YOU KNOW?

The combined gross domestic product of the poorest forty-eight nations is less than the wealth of the world's three richest people combined.

(source: Globalissues.org)

Unleashing the Killer Bee Within

So, you still feel like a tiny, insignificant bee in a gigantic hive, toiling away endlessly with no end in sight? Well, maybe you are. And maybe you will be there for a very long time. The choice is entirely yours. You can convince yourself that you have to stay, or you can convince yourself that you have to move on. But regardless of whether you stay for a month or a decade, the single most important question remains the same. Are you using the job or is it using you?

Get Pimpin'

For many of us our jobs are a means by which we sustain ourselves while working toward larger personal goals. For others the job may provide much needed security for a family or a chance to improve the lives of our children. And for some a steady job means independence from a bad situation. For the luckiest among us the job itself provides creative fulfillment and a deep sense of pride. But if the job is sucking you dry, draining your energies, and squashing your spirit, then you are the one being used. Resentment, bitterness, and general unhappiness are inevitable when we feel that we are underappreciated, taken for granted, or living beneath our potential. And if that's the case, it is your responsibility to make a change.

Beyond the question of who's using whom, there are others to ponder. Are you easily replaced, or is your employer easily replaced? Do you live to work, or do you work to live? Are you really setting a good example for your kids if you are living a life of misery? These little distinctions make all the difference in the world. In a tough situation change is not always easy, but it is always worth consideration, and you'll never recognize opportunity if your eyes are closed to possibility. You must know by now that at every step of life, you do have a choice. And choosing to do nothing is in itself a choice.

So, what do you want out of your life? Do you already have it? Will your income help you to realize it? Is your job preventing you from achieving it? Or are you actually happy and fulfilled in your current job? Can you begin to work toward your dream today without quitting your job? Should you make a clean break and jump into the deep end of the unknown? You already know the answers to all of these questions. Just ask yourself: "What do I really want?"

In the meantime, as long as you continue to shovel away, remember:

▲ Nothing in life is permanent.

▲ There is comedy to be found in all situations.

▲ Friends can make the unbearable bearable.

▲ You are in control of your own stress levels.

▲ Sleeping well is the key to sanity.

▲ Zen is the state of perfect balance.

▲ Never give up on your creative passions.

▲ You're better off than Earl.

Now get back to work. ;-)

A MEMO ON THE TYPE:

This book is set in various typefaces
from the Swiss 721 family, which was created
by Bitstream Inc. as an updated, standardized
version of the classic Helvetica font.

Thank you for your attention.
Please resume your office duties.